How to achieve a C and above in
GCSE AQA A ENGLISH

Peter Buckroyd
Chief Examiner for GCSE English

www.heinemann.co.uk

✓ Free online support
✓ Useful weblinks
✓ 24 hour online ordering

01865 888118

Heinemann is an imprint of Pearson Education Limited, a company incorporated in England and Wales, having its registered office at Edinburgh Gate, Harlow, Essex, CM20 2JE. Registered company number: 872828

www.heinemann.co.uk

Text © Pearson Education Limited 2008

First published 2008

12 11 10 09 08

10 9 8 7 6 5 4 3 2 1

British Library Cataloguing in Publication Data is available from the British Library on request.

ISBN 978 0 435118 58 7

Websites

The websites used in this book were correct and up-to-date at the time of publication. It is essential for tutors to preview each website before using it in class so as to ensure that the URL is still accurate, relevant and appropriate.

Designed by Tony Richardson (Wooden Ark, Leeds)

Produced by Wooden Ark

Original illustrations © Pearson Education Limited 2008

Illustrated by Rory Walker

Cover design by Tony Richardson (Wooden Ark, Leeds)

Picture research by Zooid Pictures Limited

Printed and bound in the UK by Scotprint

Acknowledgements

The author and publisher would like to thank the following individuals and organisations for permission to reproduce photographs:

pp9, 45 Jim Reed/Robert Harding World Imagery/Digital Vision; p11 Sally A. Morgan; Ecoscene/CORB/Corbis UK Ltd; p14 Hotel OMM; p15 Stu Forster/Allsport/Getty Images; p16 Digital Vision; p24 Peter Luckhurst; p29 Rosie Greenway/Getty Images; p32 Construction Photography/Corbis UK Ltd; pp39, 40 Nicholas Hendrickx/Barcroft Media; p42 Digfoto/Imagebroker/FLPA/Frank Lane Picture Agency; pp44, 71 Photolibrary Group; p45 (top) Hulton-Deutsch Collection/Corbis UK Ltd; p51 Photo by Hulton Archive/Getty Images; p54 PA Archive/PA Photos; p56 Travelshots.com/Alamy; p62 RubberBall/Alamy; p72 Helene Rogers/Alamy; p73 Playboy Archive/Corbis UK Ltd; p75 Raj Patidar/Reuters/Corbis UK Ltd; p83 Geoff Kidd/Science Photo Library; p84 Kevin Cooley/Getty Images; p87 Rex Features/Rex Features; p88 PhotosIndia.com LLC/Alamy; p92 Getty Images; p99 Boryana Katsarova/AFP/Getty Images; p102 Gary Irving/Digital Vision; p 107 Alan Schein Photography/Corbis UK Ltd; p109 PA WIRE/PA Photos; p112 Chris Jackson/Getty Images; p117 Andrew Crowley/Daily Telegraph; p119 BBC Wales/Patrick Olner; p120 PhotoDisc; p123 MedioImages/Alamy Images; p124 PhotoDisc; p125 ImageState/Alamy; pp131, 137 Brian David Stevens/Corbis UK Ltd; p141 JOSE LUIS ROCA/AFP/Getty Images; p142 Julie Mowbray/Alamy; p145 ImageState/Alamy; p147 Steve Bloom Images/Alamy; pp157, 161 David Cloud/iStockphoto.

Every effort has been made to contact copyright holders of material reproduced in this book. Any omissions will be rectified in subsequent printings if notice is given to the publishers.

Article 'Mr Men are given a makeover' by Amol Rajan, *The Independent*, 18th October, 2007. © *The Independent* 2007. Reprinted with permission; use of the front page from *The Times*, 24 July 2007. © NI Syndication 2007. Reprinted with permission (photograph © SWNS – reprinted with permission); front page from *The Daily Mirror*, January 11 2007. Reprinted with permission of Mirrorpix; small extract about Hotel OMM, Barcelona, from www.i-escape.com. Reprinted with permission; article 'Dario on the Boos', *News of the World*, 23rd September, 2007. Copyright © NI Syndications 2007. Reprinted with permission; article 'Record ice-melt in Arctic', *The Times*, Saturday 22nd October, 2007. Copyright © NI Syndications 2007. Reprinted with permission; 'Give your immune system a boost' by Jeannette Jackson. Copyright © Jeannette Jackson. Reprinted with the kind permission of the author; weather forecast map and text, *The Times*, Tuesday 16th October, 2007. © NI Sydications 2007. Reprinted with permission; article 'A rare chance to beat the inflation beast' by Jo Thornhill, *The Mail on Sunday*, September 30 2007. Reprinted with permission of Solo Syndication; article 'Swear Works: 4 letter blast good for staff' by Aidan McGurran, *The Daily Mirror*, October 17 2007. Reprinted with permission of Trinity Mirror, Mirrorpix; 'Modern Morals' from *Should I flush my goldfish down the loo?* by Joe Joseph, published by Hodder & Stoughton. Reprinted with permission of Hodder & Stoughton; extract from 'Understanding British Buildings' by Carole Machin, in *A Visitor's Britain: Exploring Culture Past and Present*, edited by Martin Upham and Patricia Tatspaugh, published by AHA International. Copyright © Carole Machin. Reprinted with the kind permission of the author; article 'The Sun Says: No defence', *The Sun*, Wednesday 17th October, 2007. Copyright © NI Syndications 2007. Logo and article reprinted with permission; article 'The fantastic Mr Fly' by Ross McGuiness, *The Metro*, 4 November 2007. Reprinted with permission of Solo Syndication; article 'Days like these – 18 October 1930', compiled by Rebecca Armstrong, *The Independent*, 18th October, 2007 © *The Independent*. Reprinted with permission'; article 'Fringe Benefits', *The Sun*, Monday 22nd October, 2007. Copyright © NI Syndication 2007. Reprinted with permission; back page of Sir John Soanes museum leaflet, from 'Short Description', reprinted by courtesy of the Trustees of Sir John Soane's Museum; article 'The Elephant Man' by Emma Morton, *The Sun*, Wednesday 17th October, 2007. Copyright © NI Syndications 2007. Reprinted with permission; extract from article 'Beautiful Britain: Need an autumn break? Look closer to home and you'll be pleasantly surprised' by Chris Alden, *The Daily Telegraph*, 18th October, 2007. Reprinted with permission; Tiny extract from 'Flight' from *Collected African Stories* by Doris Lessing. Copyright © Doris Lessing 1957. Reprinted by kind permission of Jonathan Clowes Ltd, London on behalf of Doris Lessing; article 'X Factor vote row', *The Times*, 18th December, 2007. Copyright © NI Syndications 2007. Reprinted with permission; 'The Present Song' by Carol Ann Duffy, from *The Manchester Carols*, December 2007. Copyright © Carol Ann Duffy 2007. Reprinted with the kind permission of the author; article 'You can't Bea that daft', *The Sun*, 18th December, 2007. Copyright © NI Syndications 2007. Reprinted with permission; 'Community Musician for Clase and Caemawr?' from December 2007 newsletter. Reprinted with permission; extract from article 'Don't write to me – my time is for God' by Peter Stanford, *The Daily Telegraph*, 18th October, 2007. Reprinted with permission; article 'Standing in a Methodist chapel....' by Hilary Freeman, *The Daily Mail*, 6 November 2007. Reprinted with permission of Solo Syndication; article 'Drunken Monkey Killed My Wife!' by Neil Goodwin, *Daily Sport*, 30 October, 2006. Reprinted with permission; Article 'India Official Dies After Monkey Attack', 21st October, 2007 Copyright © The Associated Press. All rights reserved. Reprinted with permission of The YGS Group; article 'Delhi battles monkey menace' by Alok Pandey, Monday 22 October 2007, NDTV. Reprinted with kind permission of NDTV Convergence.

Contents

Introduction

How does this book work?

This book is designed to help students raise their achievement in GCSE AQA A English from a D grade to a C or B. It aims to do this by focusing on the Paper 1 and Paper 2 exam requirements.

The book breaks down the Assessment Objectives into their component parts. The book then shows how the Assessment Objectives cross over between Paper 1 and Paper 2. Additionally, it provides students with:

- guidance and teaching on the key skills that make the difference between a D and a C grade
- examples of students' work at grades D and C with examiner comments
- activities that allow students to reflect and improve on their learning
- the relevant mark scheme descriptors together with guidance on what the examiners are looking for
- hints from the Chief Examiner on how to move from a D to a C and then to a B.

The approach that this book uses comes out of many years of examining experience and out of workshops, training sessions and revision courses with teachers and students. It can be used with confidence by all Foundation or Higher tier students who need to move from a grade D to a grade C (and then to a grade B).

Throughout the book there are opportunities for peer- and self-assessment. In addition, not only are students encouraged to reflect on what they have learnt, but they are also given ideas for how they can continue to practise and revise for their two GCSE English exams.

Finally, at the end of the book are four sample exam papers. These are examples of Paper 1 and Paper 2 exams at both Foundation and Higher levels, and can be used at any time in the course.

The AQA A GCSE English exams

Paper 1

What is this exam worth?	30% of the total marks
How long is this exam?	1¾ hours
What is Section A of the exam?	Reading response to non-fiction/media texts
What is Section A worth?	15% of the total marks
What is Section B of the exam?	Choice of one from four questions testing writing that seeks to argue, persuade or advise
What is Section B worth?	15% of the total marks

Paper 2

What is this exam worth?	30% of the total marks
How long is this exam?	1½ hours
What is Section A of the exam?	Reading response to poetry from Different Cultures and Traditions in the AQA A Anthology
What is Section A worth?	15% of the total marks
What is Section B of the exam?	Choice of one from four questions testing writing that seeks to inform, explain or describe
What is Section B worth?	15% of the total marks

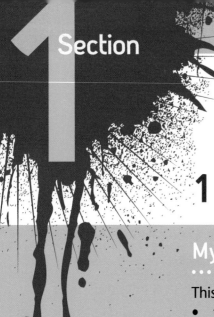

Reading

1 Read, support, develop

My learning

This chapter will help you to:
- think about what you are doing when you are reading
- show you that the same Assessment Objectives are tested in Paper 1 and Paper 2
- see that this Assessment Objective is tested in every question you answer in Section A of both papers.

Assessment Objectives

- Read with insight and engagement.
- Make appropriate references to texts.
- Develop and sustain interpretations of them.

What you are being asked to do

The skills that are being tested in the exam are the same in Paper 1 when you are writing about unseen non-fiction and media texts and in Paper 2 when you are writing about poetry.

In the exam the questions you will get on both papers will ask very similar things. What you learn in one part of the course should be used in other parts of the course, too. Begin thinking about the skills rather than the content and you will already be laying the foundations for moving from a D grade to a C or better.

Read with insight and engagement

The first part of this Assessment Objective means that the examiner can tell that you are reading carefully and thinking about what you are reading. In addition, you should show (at least for the time that the exam lasts, pretending if you have to) that you are interested in what you read.

It also means reading the questions you are asked with the same care and attention that you read the texts. The most important thing is that you don't just pay attention to **what** is said. **How** it is said is just as important, and this is a large part of what you study during your English GCSE course.

Paper 1

Activity 1

Read the following newspaper article.

Mr Men are given a makeover

By Amol Rajan

Thirty-six years after they first appeared on bookshelves, the Mr Men have had a makeover – and some have even changed sex. The children's favourites, along with their female counterparts, the Little Misses, will have their first new television outing in a decade from January. The original cast of 83 characters has been trimmed to 25 for use in the 26 new episodes launching on Five.

However, Mr Men purists may not be amused to find some of the original stars have had their genders changed to 'create balance' among the 25 that survived the cull. Others, such as Mr Lazy, appear much thinner than their predecessors, while Mr Fussy, for example, has been renamed Mr Persnickety.

John Collins of Chorion – the company which bought the rights to the brands in 2004 – said: 'We've mixed and matched opposite personalities who, when put together, will create hilarious comedy and appeal to young boys and girls.'

From *The Independent*, 18 October 2007

Jot down some points in answer to the following question:

In your own words, say what has happened to the Mr Men over 36 years.

Check your answer

- How many different points were you able to make?
- Were you able to use some of your own words?
- Were you able to draw your material from the whole of the article?

Make appropriate references to texts

A basic requirement of the exam is that you support what you have to say by close reference to, or quotation from, the texts. Of course these references or quotations need to be relevant to what you are saying. In the exam, students often quote at length, but what they are quoting doesn't fit at all clearly with the point they are making. This is often because their quotations are too long or their point is so vague that they can't find anything specific to support it.

Try to find just the right quotation to support your point. The most effective quotations are the very brief ones that examiners call 'embedded'.

For example,

The writer shows how the number of characters has been reduced from 83 to 25 by using the word 'trimmed'.

is much more precise than

The writer shows there are not so many characters: 'The original cast of 83 characters has been trimmed to 25 for use in the 26 new episodes launching on Five'.

Activity 2

Remind yourself of your answer to Activity 1. For each of the points you jotted down in Activity 1, find a precise example from the Mr Men newspaper article on page 7 that you could quote to support your point.

Activity 3

Now look at the language used in the Mr Men newspaper article and jot down some points you could make to answer the following question:

How does the language used in the article show people's points of view?

Support each point you make by including a brief quotation in the sentence you are writing.

Paper 2

You will be tested on exactly the same skills in Paper 2 on the Poems from Different Cultures and Traditions. There you will also be asked to read, to support and to develop your points.

Activity 4

Three students have written about the Different Cultures poem 'Hurricane Hits England'. Read the extracts below and answer the following questions for each one.

1 How precise is the point they are making?

2 How well does the quotation fit the point?

3 Which is the most effective and why?

Which one manages to 'embed' the quotation in the argument?

Student A

> Grace Nichols shows what effect the storm has:
>
> The blinding illumination,
> Even as you short-
> Circuit us
> Into further darkness?

Student B

> Grace Nichols thinks first about language but then considers what the storm actually does. The lightning is described as a 'blinding illumination' which creates power cuts and more darkness.

Student C

> After writing about the difficulty of adjusting to a new place where 'old tongues', those of her origin, make her feel chaotic in a new place, she goes on to see the hurricane's lightning, the 'blinding illumination', as a metaphor for the 'darkness' she feels in her new home.

What did the examiner think?

Student A left everything up to the reader. We are not told what effect the storm had and we don't know which words in the quotation have led to which thought.

Student B makes a comment about two stanzas and makes a link between language and the hurricane, but without saying what that link is. The brief quotation, though, does allow the reader to know which bit of the poem they are thinking of.

Student C 'embeds' the quotations in the sentence and also makes precise links between the two parts of the poem they are writing about. This is the best of the three responses. It links ideas and begins to offer an interpretation of part of the poem.

What you need to do

So, from the examiner's advice above you should:

- try to get used to using quotations and close references that are no longer than you need them to be
- choose a reference or quotation that fits the point as precisely as possible
- try to 'embed' your quotations in the sentence, so that the reader knows what you are thinking about but also so that your argument doesn't have to stop while you make a quotation.

Paper 1 and Paper 2
Develop and sustain interpretations

We have seen how Student C above, even in a very short extract, was beginning to develop an interpretation of part of the poem. 'Develop' really means link different things together and allow one point to follow on from the previous one. 'Sustain' means 'keep it going'.

You need to do this both in Paper 1 and in Paper 2. So think again about the Mr Men article on page 7 and about the Different Cultures poem 'Hurricane Hits England' from your Anthology.

Activity 5

Answer the following question on the Mr Men article (page 7). You can build on the points that you found when you did Activity 1.

What changes have happened to the Mr Men over the last 36 years and why? Support the points you make by reference to details in the text.

Check your answer

- Did you make a range of points?
- Did you answer both 'what' and 'why'?
- Did you embed your quotations?

The skills are just the same when writing about the Poems from Different Cultures. Look carefully at what Student C went on to write after the brief extract in Activity 4. The student is continuing to write about the poem 'Hurricane Hits England'.

She then considers a wider perspective. The hurricane has brought down trees, but because she is thinking about a sea passage this reminds her that their weight might be 'as heavy as whales'. She goes on to think that where the trees have been uprooted are craters. At the end of the poem she applies these trees to herself. She has been uprooted just as the trees have and this allows her to come to the realisation that no matter whether in the Caribbean or England, the 'earth' is the same. Perhaps she is implying that she, too, is the same whichever country she is in.

Activity 6

Look at the extract above and find the places where the student:

1. makes points
2. uses textual detail to support the points
3. embeds a quotation
4. develops and sustains an interpretation.

What did the examiner think?

It doesn't matter whether you agree with this interpretation of the poem 'Hurricane Hits England'. This student is explaining their own interpretation, and is using very short quotations and references to details of the text to support and develop their response to it.

What you need to do

So, from the examiner's advice above you should:

- try to link points together
- try to write about parts of the poem in the light of the whole poem
- get to know the poems as well as you can by reading them for yourself several times. The more familiar the details will then be, the easier it will be for you to think about making, developing and sustaining interpretations of them.

What have I learnt?

Check that you:

- know what the examiners are looking for
- practise using quotations to support the points you make
- use quotations that are no longer than they need to be to support the point you are making
- read the poems for yourself several times
- begin to link things together to make interpretations.

In the future you:

- can increase your skill in making good quotations and close references
- can read the poems for yourself to become really familiar with them. If you just read two every day, think how little time that would take and how well you would know them by the time the exam came.

2 Fact and opinion

My learning

This chapter will help you to:
- select facts and opinions from a passage
- comment on the writer's use of fact and opinion
- write about facts and opinions in the exam
- improve your written response.

Assessment Objective

- Distinguish between fact and opinion.

In the exam you will be asked to select facts and opinions, or comment on a writer's use of facts and opinions. So, it is important that you understand the difference between facts and opinions.

Getting started

To show that you know how to distinguish between facts and opinions, make sure you know the following:
- Facts are pieces of information that are true. You can check them out to see if they are really true. For example, it is a fact that Madrid is the capital of Spain.
- Opinions are what people think. For example, 'Manchester United is the best football team in the world', is an opinion.

> ### Examiner hints
> - Don't write down more words than you need to.
> - Try to pick the most obvious examples of facts and opinions.
> - If the question asks you for your own words, then rephrase what is in the passage.
> - If it asks you to select, then you can pick out and copy.

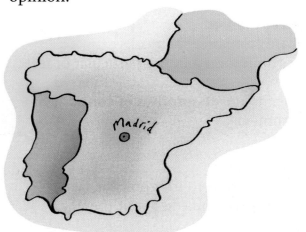

Activity 1

Select and write down two facts and two opinions from the following newspaper article.

HOTEL OMM, BARCELONA

Close to Gaudi's apartment block, Casa Milà, this trendy hotel is in the heart of the city near the busy Passeig de Gràcia. There are 91 rooms with floor-to-ceiling panels of glass and American oak floors. The Moo Restaurant serves up its own version of Catalan cuisine.

Bonus: Take a dip in the rooftop pool.
Drawback: High-tech gadgetry can be a bit overwhelming.
Book it: www.i-escape.com/hotelomm.php.

Rooms from £260 a night, excluding breakfast and flights.

From *The Times* (Travel), 22 September 2007

Check your answer

- Have you made clear which you think are facts and which are opinions?
- Have you selected the most **obvious** facts?
- Have you selected what are **clearly** opinions?

Some sorts of writing involve only facts. Some involve only opinions. But most contain a mixture of both. Once you can identify straightforward facts and straightforward opinions, you can begin to look at how writers use them.

There may be many different uses of facts and opinions.

Facts might be used to:
- support the writer's opinion
- persuade, bombard, convince the reader
- make the reader think something in particular or feel something
- confuse the reader, to create surprises or contrasts or contradictions/ironies.

Opinions might:
- be used to argue a case
- guide the reader about how to interpret the facts, by coming to a particular conclusion about them.

Activity 2

1   First of all, identify all the facts and all the opinions in the following newspaper article.

2   How many facts are there and how many opinions?

3   Explain how each of the facts and opinions is used. You might start with the names of the players (facts) and the first quotation from Gradi (opinion). This will make you think about the writer's purposes or about the particular bias or point of view being presented.

DARIO ON THE BOOS

CREWE 0   MILLWALL 0

CREWE boss Dario Gradi admitted he was happy to pinch a point from a dire scrap.

Boos rang out around Gresty Road as the stuttering Railwaymen failed to impress against the lowly Lions.

Gradi said: "The fans were fair. They didn't boo during the game.

"The team gave their best but people think we should be beating sides like Millwall because they are below us. But they are a big club compared to us.

"A draw is not a disaster and we didn't want to throw caution to the wind with 10 minutes to go and risk losing the game in the dying seconds.

"I think the crowd wanted a bit more blood-and-thunder but I don't think blood-and-thunder was going to win the game today."

A draw was more satisfying for the Lions, who battled hard to end their five-game losing streak.

Watford frontman Will Hoskins was brought in on a month's loan to add some sting to an attack that has scored only three league goals this season.

But the 21-year-old blew the chance to score two minutes into his debut, drilling into the side netting from 10 yards before being subbed after an hour.

Crewe rarely threatened but Danny Woodards nearly won it two minutes from time, stinging the hands of Rab Douglas with a 25-yard piledriver.

From *News of the World* (Score) 23 September 2007

Check your answer

* Did you notice how few facts there were?
* Did you see how emotive some of the opinions were?
* There are different sorts of opinions here – those of the writer, the crowd, the Crewe manager and the Millwall supporters.
* Facts are used to inform – the score, the name of Crewe's football ground, Millwall's nickname, three players' names, the age of one player.
* Opinions are used to make the match report seem lively, interesting, entertaining and emotional.

Examiner hints

• Make sure you include specific facts and opinions from the text when you are writing about their uses.

• Try to have an overview as well as writing in detail.

You have about 10 minutes to answer each of the questions on this part of the exam, so you need an efficient technique. Before you answer the question:

• underline or highlight the facts and the opinions as you come across them when reading the article

• make a brief pencil note about the use of each of them. It might help to think about the writer's purposes.

Activity 3

Now look at the ways facts and opinions are used in the following newspaper article by answering the question below, which is one that you might be asked in the exam:

How are facts and opinions used in this passage? You should spend about 10 minutes on this.

Record ice-melt in Arctic

Ice in the Arctic has retreated at such a record rate that the fabled North-west Passage route, around the top of North America, opened up and became fully navigable for around five weeks (Lewis Smith writes).

The speed of the retreat shown by satellites has astonished scientists, who say that this year's melt beat the record by an area five times the size of the UK. Scientists from the University of Colorado measured the minimum extent of the Arctic ice as being 1.59 million square miles (4.13 million square km) on September 16. It broke the record set on September 20 in 2005 by an area of 460,000 square miles.

Sea ice in the Arctic is beginning to freeze again with the approach of winter and researchers said

that any further retreat this year was unlikely.

Global warming was cited as the main factor in the extent of the ice loss along with natural variability. Rising concentrations of greenhouse gases have, they said, increased temperatures across the region.

Scientists at the university's National Snow and Ice Data Centre forecast that at current rates, the Arctic could be ice-free in the summer by 2030.

John Sauven, of Greenpeace, said: 'The canary in the coal mine is singing very loudly now. At this rate we could see the end of summer sea ice in our lifetimes.'

From *The Times*, 22 September 2007

....

Check your answer

• Did you use specific facts in your answer?

• Did you use specific opinions?

• Did you have an overall idea about how they were used?

• Did you link the facts and opinions to the writer's overall purposes?

What the examiners are looking for

Read the following answer to the task on page 16, written by a student. Then read the examiner comments around the text and at the end.

Two facts linked

Attempts comment on use, though very vague

> The writer mentions facts about the size of the Arctic ice (1.59 million miles and 460,000 square miles) in order to make the reader believe in what he is saying. John Sauven's opinion is used to make people understand that Greenpeace and other interested parties care about the ice melting.

Mentions opinion but doesn't quote it

Attempts comment on use

What did the examiner think?

This student doesn't extend his comments; one point does not lead him to develop it or to link it with a further point. It has some of the characteristics of the **D/E** band, but it is brief and rather generalised.

Activity 4

Answer the following questions to see how the student's answer above could be improved.

1 What extra points could the student make?
2 For these extra points, how could the student:
   • link and develop them
   • mention more facts
   • mention more opinions
   • comment on the uses of each of them?

Sometimes there are complications in dealing with fact and opinion. For instance (looking back at the article on page 16), it is a fact (because you could look up whether it was true or not) that scientists at the university's National Snow and Ice Data Centre forecast that 'at current rates, the Arctic could be ice-free in the summer by 2030'. However, it isn't a fact that the Arctic will be ice-free by 2030. That is their opinion, based on their research, and it is the words 'could be' that tell us this.

Activity 5

Now check your own answer to Activity 3 by applying the mark scheme below, which the examiner would be using. There are two bands of marks, covering Grades E–B. You will need to be careful and precise in your marking.

D/E – 'some awareness'	B/C – 'clear attempt to select'
• some extended supported comment • unstructured response that tends to paraphrase • some identification of facts and opinions • some awareness of uses.	• clear and effective attempt to engage with task • structured response • selects and comments on uses • a range of examples of uses of facts and uses of opinions.

What have I learnt?

Check that you:

• know about facts, opinions and their uses
• know what the examiners are looking for.

In the future you:

• can practise on your own with any pieces of writing you come across, such as newspaper articles, magazine articles, pages from textbooks, letters and advertisements.

3 How information is presented

My learning

This chapter will help you to:

- identify what kind of information is given
- comment on the methods used to present the information
- make judgements about how effective these methods are
- improve your written response.

Assessment Objective

- Evaluate how information is presented.

In the exam you might be asked to comment on how effectively or how well information is presented in a particular text. In order to do this it's important to know what sorts of things to look for.

Getting started

In order to evaluate how information is presented, make sure you know:

- what sorts of information you are looking at
- the purpose of the information
- its audience
- how it is organised
- what kinds of language it uses
- what kinds of presentational devices it uses
- how successfully you think it does each of these things.

Read the article on page 20, then complete Activity 1.

Give your immune system a boost ...

Want to look and feel young, fresh and healthy, without spending a fortune? It's time to take care of your immune system.

IT MAY NOT SOUND SEXY BUT YOUR IMMUNE SYSTEM IS INTEGRAL TO ALL THAT YOU ARE AND ALL THAT YOU DO.

If you want to look young, fresh and healthy with a glow that you can't buy from a bottle then it's a good idea to learn about how to keep your immune system strong and virulent.

THE SCIENCE BIT

The immune system enables us to resist infections and it can be separated into two functional components:

The innate system is implicated primarily in the body's first form of defence. The majority of infections caused by invading pathogens typically occur within the mucous membranes of the body which offer peripheral protection by way of the skin, cilia, tears, nasal secretions and saliva, all of which orchestrate an elaborate tiered structure to keep extraneous nasties out.

The adaptive immune system acts as a second line of defence and also affords protection against re-exposure to the same pathogen.

OVER TO YOU

You are exposed to pathogens all day every day so it's wise to do everything you can to boost your immune system as it literally can make the difference between life or death in some instances. The easiest way to boost your innate immune system is by working on your diet so your propensity to 'catch' a cold or infection is reduced. Certain foods contain components that enhance immune function in a variety of ways and when included regularly into your diet can work wonders on your defence system.

However you also need to address certain lifestyle aspects as well such as stress and sleep.

SO WHERE DO YOU START?

The following superfoods need to be a must in your diet each week as they are the most immune supporting foods around:

Red peppers These provide 450% of daily Vitamin C quota

Avocado Packed with the most powerful antioxidant Vitamin E

Spinach High in Vitamin A which is known as the 'Anti-Infection' vitamin

Papaya Helps boost white blood cell count and lowers nasal congestion

Walnuts Good source of copper for healthy immune system plus lowers cholesterol

Jeanette Jackson

Jeanette Jackson is a Stress and Nutrition Expert who specialises in on-line nutrition and diet programmes.

From *Out North West* magazine, October 2007

Read the article opposite. Then complete Activity 1.

Activity 1

Read the article on page 20 about healthy eating. While you are reading it, jot down the different kinds of information that you are given.

Activity 2

Your answer to Activity 1 might have included information about:

- the article's purpose
- the immune system
- what you can do about your immune system
- 'superfoods'
- the nutrition expert.

Now make a list of the different methods that are used to present the information in the article on page 20. Try to link each one with a specific piece of information:

- colour
- print size
- print style
- organisational devices
- layout
- kinds of language (how formal is the language?).

Examiner hints

- Make sure each point you make is supported with a precise example.
- Make sure you comment on the effectiveness of each of the things you choose to write about.
- Aim for five different points.

Now you have the information on which your judgements are to be based, you need to think about how effectively you think the information is presented. For example, if you identify what you think is the writer's purpose, then you can think about how well she achieved this purpose.

The examiner wants to see what you've noticed and what you think about it. A good answer is going to be one that:
- makes about five different points
- uses specific detail from the passage
- supports the judgements by reference to that detail.

It's not how correct your judgement is that counts, but the thinking that has gone on behind it. You need to be able to observe the precise detail and support what you have to say convincingly.

Activity 3

Now write an answer for 10 minutes on the following question:

How effectively do you think information is presented in the article on page 20?

Remember to include:

- the kinds of information contained in the article
- the different methods used to present the information
- how effectively the first two bullets above are presented.

For further help, remind yourself of the 'Getting started' list on page 19.

The text you have just looked at consisted only of text. Quite often, however, writers use different techniques to get their information across. Sometimes they use other devices in order to make the information more attractive or interesting, particularly if it is rather dry. The example you have just analysed, though, also used some devices to break up the text, such as the different coloured capitalised headings and the emboldened names of the superfoods.

The two texts that follow use quite different methods to make their information more attractive than it would have been, had it appeared in a block of continuous writing. The first is a weather forecast from a newspaper, giving information people want about weather conditions. The second is giving information to people who have some money about how to make good use of it in investments.

Read the two pieces. Then complete Activity 4 that follows.

Today heavy rain in the South. Max 16C (61F), min 2C (36F)

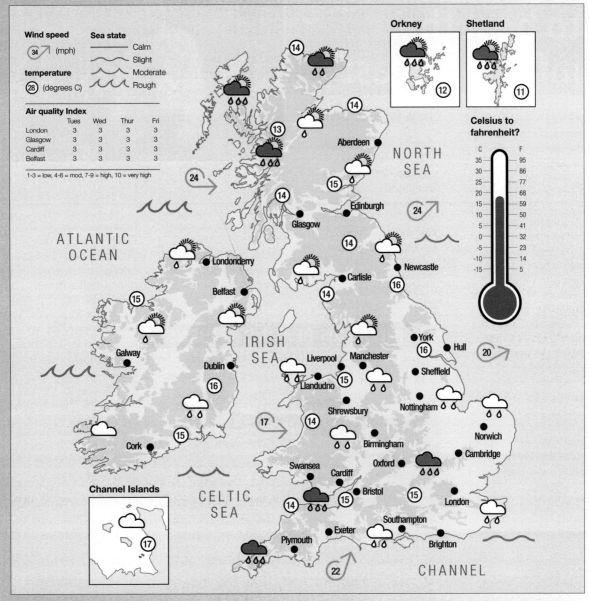

Wind speed
34 (mph)

temperature
28 (degrees C)

Sea state
— Calm
~ Slight
~~ Moderate
~~~ Rough

Air quality Index

	Tues	Wed	Thur	Fri
London	3	3	3	3
Glasgow	3	3	3	3
Cardiff	3	3	3	3
Belfast	3	3	3	3

1-3 = low, 4-6 = mod, 7-9 = high, 10 = very high

Orkney 12 **Shetland** 11

Celsius to fahrenheit?

C	F
35	95
30	86
25	77
20	68
15	59
10	50
5	41
0	32
-5	23
-10	14
-15	5

NORTH SEA

Aberdeen 15

Edinburgh 14

Glasgow 14

Newcastle 16

York 16 Hull 20

Carlisle 14

ATLANTIC OCEAN

Londonderry 15

Belfast 15

Galway 15

Dublin 16

IRISH SEA

Liverpool Manchester
Llandudno 15 Sheffield
Shrewsbury 14 Nottingham

Cork 15

Birmingham 15

Norwich

Cambridge

Swansea 14 Oxford 15
Cardiff 15 Bristol London 15

CELTIC SEA

Exeter Southampton
Plymouth Brighton

Channel Islands 17

CHANNEL

24 24 20 17 22

General situation: Rain will affect the South of England, heavy in the South West, becoming more persistent in the East later. Drier in the North with a few showers.

SW Eng, Wales: Dull and wet with a lengthy spell of heavy rain. Light or moderate southwesterly wind. Maximum 15C (59F), minimum 9C (48F).

Cen S Eng, Midlands, E Anglia: A cloudy start with patchy rain, becoming heavier and persistent later. Wind light or moderate southwesterly. Maximum 15C (59F), minimum 7C (45F)

London, SE Eng, Channel Is: Starting cloudy with light rain at times, but this becoming a little more persistent late in the day. Moderate southwesterly wind. Maximum 15C (59F), minimum 10C (50F).

N Ireland, Republic of Ireland, N Eng, IoM, Lake District, Borders, SW Scotland, Edinburgh and Dundee, Aberdeen: Sunny spells, but a fair amount of cloud at times bringing mostly isolated showers. Wind moderate to fresh west or southwesterly. Maximum 16C (61F), minimum 3C (37F).

Argyll, Glasgow, Cen Highland, NW Scotland, Moray Firth, NE Scotland, N Isles: Bright or sunny spells, but rather cloudy at times bringing scattered, blustery and heavy showers. Fresh west or southwesterly wind. Maximum 14C (57F), minimum 2C (36F).

From *The Times*, 16 October 2007

A rare chance to beat the inflation beast

Priority: Peter Ankers insists on a rate that beats inflation

INFLATION is the deadly enemy of savers, eating into the interest rate they earn on cash deposits.

At present, inflation is 4.1 per cent as measured by the Retail Prices Index. This means that people paying the basic-rate tax of 20 per cent on savings must earn at least 5.12 per cent simply to keep pace. This rises to 6.83 per cent for higher-rate taxpayers.

Unusually, at present, there are rates available at these high levels, but they may disappear.

National Savings & Investments' Index-linked Savings Certificates offer inflation-beating returns, free of income or capital gains tax. The certificates, offered over three or five

By Jo Thornhill

years, pay a guaranteed 1.35 per cent above inflation. The minimum investment is £100 and the maximum is £15,000, but savers must lock their cash away for the term. Encashment in the first year will lead to the loss of all interest and index-linking.

The RPI, measured by the Office of National Statistics, changes monthly so savers won't know exactly how much they have earned on their savings until maturity. But the value of their money has kept ahead of rising prices. Interest is calculated and compounded monthly.

Sue Hannums of financial adviser AWD Chase de Vere in Bath, Somerset, says: 'National Savings' index-linked products offer fantastic value. The equivalent rates would be 6.81 per cent for a basic-rate taxpayer or 9.08 per cent on the higher rate.'

Peter Ankers, a retired finance manager from Woking, Surrey, invested in a three-year index-linked savings certificate with NS&I. 'My priorities are that my money is secure and the rate is beating inflation,' he says.

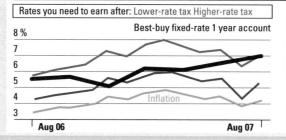

INFLATION-BEATING RETURNS

Rates you need to earn after: Lower-rate tax Higher-rate tax

Best-buy fixed-rate 1 year account

Inflation

Aug 06   Aug 07

From *The Mail on Sunday*, 30 September 2007

Activity 4

Looking carefully at the two texts, with the 'Getting started' list (on page 19) in mind, copy and complete the following table. Try to put in as many points as you can – some have been done for you.

	Different kinds of information	**Different kinds of language/ presentational devices**
Weather forecast	Temperature Rain	
Financial text		Picture Graph

Activity 5

For each of the two texts on pages 23 and 24, write a 10-minute answer to this question:

How effectively do you think information is presented in this item?

Read Student A's answer below together with the examiner's comments around it and after it. Then complete Activity 6 that follows.

Student A: Weather forecast

Comment on effectiveness, qualified

Analysis of effectiveness

Comment on effectiveness

Range of information

Evaluation
Method

Two methods

Clear comment on language

Range of content

Comment on effectiveness

The information on the map is very clear, although there is no key to the clouds and raindrops. It leaves the reader to assume that in places where there are three raindrops it means that it will be three times wetter than where there is only one raindrop. It is very clear where there might be some sunshine. The map includes city names, a temperature diagram and an air quality index. The unlabelled map of the Channel Isles is a bit puzzling to those who are not very familiar with that part of the world. The writing underneath the map looks much denser and seems to repeat the information much more clearly presented on the map. It is mainly in note form with verbless sentences. It is the sort of fragmented language often used on radio or television weather forecasts. This item uses conventions very familiar to those who look at weather forecasts: a map, clouds, raindrops, place names, thermometer and generalised regional descriptions in prose. It is visually varied and clearly presented in a box.

Method

What did the examiner think?

This is a very good answer which makes a range of points, makes clear evaluations and supports its points with precise details from the text.

Activity 6

Has Student A:

1 made several different points
2 referred to language
3 referred to presentational devices
4 made judgements
5 supported what they have to say with precise details?

Provide examples to support your answers.

Now read Student B's answer below, together with the examiner's comments and the mark scheme. Then complete Activity 7.

Student B: Beating inflation

General comment —

Content —

Comment on effectiveness —

Extended comment —

Comment on effectiveness —

Method, effect, purpose —

The heading is clear and easy to understand. There is a lot of information about investments here and lots of figures. It is quite hard to read because it assumes that the reader knows about finance and investments and it uses words that are not familiar. The graph is not very easy to understand except that the 'Best-buy fixed-rate 1 year accounts' are emphasised. The writer makes it less heavy by a picture of an old man.

What did the examiner think?

Let's look at the mark scheme that the examiners would be using to mark this response.

D/E	B/C
• some extended supported comment • unstructured response which tends to paraphrase • some identification of methods of presentation • some detailed comment on effectiveness.	• clear and effective attempt to engage with the task • structured response • selects and comments on methods of presentation • range of evaluations based on precise detail.

This answer meets all the D/E descriptors but only begins to meet the third descriptor in the B/C band.

Activity 7

Has Student B done the following?

1 Made several different points?
2 Referred to language?
3 Referred to presentational devices?
4 Made judgements?
5 Supported what they have to say with precise details?

Provide examples to support your answers.

Activity 8

Finally, re-read your answers from Activity 5. Try to apply the mark scheme descriptors above to your own answers and see where you could have made improvements.

What have I learnt?

Check that you:

• know what to write about in order to evaluate how information is presented
• know what the examiners are looking for
• can use the mark scheme descriptors to help you make sure that you produce work in the higher band.

In the future you:

• can practise this skill on your own with any pieces of informative writing you come across.

4 Follow an argument

My learning

This chapter will help you to:
- follow an argument
- pick out main points
- improve your written response in the exam.

Assessment Objective

- Follow an argument.

What you are being asked to do

This Assessment Objective can be tested on Paper 1. It won't be tested on Paper 2. However, in order to understand the Different Cultures poems, tested in Paper 2, you need to be able to follow what is written in the poems. Therefore, it is helpful to think about this Assessment Objective for Paper 2 as well as for Paper 1.

There are various different ways this Assessment Objective might be tested in the Paper 1 exam. You might be asked to pick out the main points in a piece of writing. You might be asked a general question which means that you have to follow the thread of a piece of writing.

You might be asked to summarise what a writer has to say. You might be asked to select points and copy them (usually on the Foundation paper) or you might be asked to select some main points and put them in your own words.

All of these question test how well you can read a piece of writing and select the main points.

Getting started

To show that you can follow an argument, make sure you:
- select specific points as you read
- highlight or underline them as you read
- identify when a new point is made
- don't include examples
- don't include repetition or different examples of the same thing
- use some of your own words when asked to do so
- summarise.

Activity 1

This newspaper article is about swearing in the workplace. As you read the article, make a list of the main points as you go along. This will help you practise how, in the exam, you can start to make notes as you are reading the text.

SWEAR WORKS

4-letter blast 'good for staff'

CURSES: Chef
Gordon Ramsay

SWEARING at work can be healthy for employees – but foul-mouthed bosses do more harm than good.

A study found workers are able to let off steam and defuse tension with a well-timed curse.

And many younger staff communicate more effectively by using four-letter words to express themselves.

But the study found managers who swear in the workplace have a negative effect, damaging morale and making employees feel bullied.

Prof Yeruda Baruch, who led the research at Norwich Business School, said the findings showed that rude bosses such as TV chef Gordon Ramsay are wrong to reprimand staff with a stream of expletives.

By Aidan McGurran

He added: 'We found employees used swearing on a continuous basis but not necessarily in a negative, abusive manner.

'Swearing was used as a social phenomenon to reflect solidarity and enhance group cohesiveness or as a psychological phenomenon to release stress.

'But it is wrong for leaders to swear at their staff because it can make people feel bullied.'

Prof Baruch, whose team studied employees and bosses at a mail order firm and questioned bankers, restaurant staff and hospital workers, said that swearing was obviously unsuitable in some professions.

He added: 'Clearly it is not right to swear if you are dealing with customers in a bank or if you are a doctor or nurse treating a patient.

TAKING THE P**S

What is considered a swearword changes with time. P**s is used in the King James Bible in preference to urinate.
2 Kings 18:27

'But when staff go back to their own room and talk among themselves it helps them to let off steam. It is not a bad thing. Although personally I don't approve of swearing.'

The survey found women swear just as much as men – and suggested a bad language ban damaged morale.

It also found staff generally only swore in areas where they could not be overheard by customers.

From the *Daily Mirror*, 17 October 2007

Activity 2

Your answer to Activity 1 might have included some of the following points.

- Swearing at work can be good for helping employees let off steam.
- But employees feel bullied if managers swear.
- Prof Yaruda Baruch's research shows that swearing is unsuitable in some professions …
- … because it is wrong to swear at customers …
- … although staff can let off steam among themselves by swearing.
- Women swear as much as men.
- Staff generally only swear when they can't be overheard by customers.
- What we call swear words also appear in the Bible.

Now use the eight points above to write an answer in full sentences, remembering to use some of your own words when you can. The question you are answering is:

What are the main points made in this article?

Examiner hint

In the exam you will probably be asked to write in continuous prose (full sentences) rather than in bullet points. Sometimes, though (usually on the Foundation Paper), you might just be asked to select points and copy them down. You can use a numbered list if you are asked to do that.

Activity 3

Read the article on page 31, in which the author Joe Joseph takes a moral issue and then gives his own response to it. The moral dilemma is printed in bold at the beginning of the item. His response then follows.

Read it carefully and make some notes on the following.

1 The main points of Joe Joseph's argument.
2 What the author might think about the argument.

Modern morals

I visit theatres in nearby towns, usually buying a ticket in advance. Recently I was so late that I queued for a £10 standby. I noticed that my fellow-queuers were far from down-at-heel and could easily afford to pay the full price (and would be the first to moan if these struggling theatres had to close). I know they are doing nothing illegal, but is their behaviour moral?

Regional theatres certainly could do with the money. It's also true that the rich could probably afford to pay full price for seats, swelling the theatre's income and freeing up standby seats for sale to playgoers who can only scrape up enough for a discounted £10 seat.

But why stop there? The rich can afford to buy the most expensive suits in a clothes store, so they shouldn't hog anything hanging on the cheaper rails, which should be reserved for those on tighter budgets. They can afford to pay full price for supermarket groceries, so should resist taking advantage of those buy-one-get-one-free offers so prized by cost-conscious shoppers. The rich should be allowed to buy only Bentleys, leaving the hatchbacks in the showroom for poorer drivers to buy. At sale time, proof of low income should be shown before entering any store.

Does any of this sound fair, let alone practicable? The theatre sells discounted standby tickets because it knows from experience that this lands more net revenue than waiting in vain, five minutes before curtain up, for someone ready to pay the ticket's face value. Someone can afford to pay £30 for a seat and still not wish to do so – though he may be happy enough to try a new play for a tenner. And who's to say he won't send the £20 he's saved to charity?

JOE JOSEPH

From *The Times*, 16 October 2007

Check your answer

Did you find the following main points of the argument?
- Rich people could probably afford to pay full price for the tickets.
- No one has to prove that they are poor before they get a bargain.
- Theatres sell cheap tickets in order to make more money.
- Richer people might be attracted by a bargain.
- No one knows what they might do with the money they have saved.

What could you find to say about what the author Joe Joseph thinks? You might have come up with the following.
- He knows some people will object to richer people getting a bargain.
- It isn't reasonable to be too high-minded.
- He understands why theatres make the offers.
- Nobody knows what people might do with the money they save; they might even give it to charity.

Read the extract on page 32, which is from an article on British buildings in a textbook on modern Britain. You might well get a passage like this in your exam, as it is factual and has an argument. After you've read it, complete Activity 4 on page 33.

One of the problems architects and town-planners face today is the difficulty of blending the old with the new in ancient cities. Merely designing new buildings in imitation of the old is a blind alley and forms no basis for innovation and visual excitement. In addition, there are strict conservation and planning controls concerning areas and buildings of historic interest.

5 City and countryside alike have winding roads that mostly seem haphazard and illogical; the exceptions are the old straight Roman roads and the new motorway systems. These meandering old roads follow cart tracks, which in turn skirted hills or followed streams, and have resulted in cities that are labyrinthine rather than logically planned. Bath is one of the few exceptions. In the eighteenth century its city council was almost despotic in its clearance
10 of the medieval town to make way for a new, planned town fit for the gentry to visit, take the medicinal waters and, consequently, to enable the townspeople to make money. The result is a harmonious, neo-classical, ordered city with wide streets and gracious squares. London and other cities do have sections that have been laid out according to a master plan. Regent's Park Terraces, designed by John Nash, are an example of a successful attempt to bring harmony and
15 grandeur to a building development within central London. In the later part of the nineteenth century, the more expensive urban development schemes, such as the Kensington area of London, featured grid-planned roads and communal gardens. Vertical living in apartment blocks did not catch on in Britain until the mid-nineteenth century and these were mostly designed as social housing experiments.

20 After the Great Fire in 1666, the City of London had a wonderful opportunity for radical replanning. Christopher Wren was employed to rebuild St Paul's Cathedral (see figure) and many other city churches after they had burnt down in the fire. He also envisaged a new city with wide streets and piazzas reminiscent
25 of Renaissance Rome. Sadly, the owners of each pre-fire plot of land wanted to reclaim their property and this only allowed for rebuilding along the narrow, winding medieval streets.

Again, there was a unique opportunity for
30 re-planning many cities after the bombing of World War Two, but the rush to get the population housed and businesses going again did not allow for this.

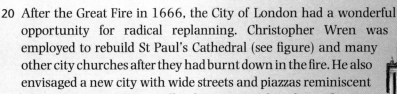

From 'Understanding British Buildings' in *A Visitor's Britain: Exploring Culture Past and Present*

Activity 4

Before you answer the question below, read the following advice.

- From the beginning, have a pencil to note what you find in the text or make notes on what you find as you read through.
- You need to decide what the author's argument is and state that clearly.
- You need to identify the different things she says.
- You need to identify the methods she uses to develop her argument.

When you have read the text on page 32 and the advice above, write a 10-minute answer to the following question:

How does Carol Machin develop her argument in this text?

What the examiners are looking for

Read the following student's response to the same task. Then read the examiner's comments around the response and after it.

> Carol Machin is writing about British cities and what they are like. She talks about how British cities and countryside are haphazard and illogical. She quotes the exceptions of Bath which was planned and some of London. She tells how after the great Fire of London and World War Two there were opportunities to replan cities.

Identifies general topic

Main point but just quoted

Part of main point – omits cities/not re-planned

What did the examiner think?

You can see that this answer does make some reference to Carol Machin's argument and that it mentions one method of developing her argument ('the exceptions'). There's very little detail of what Carol Machin says, though, and some of the points are just quotations from the text ('how British cities and countryside are haphazard and illogical').

The following is the kind of mark scheme an examiner might have if this were a question set in the exam.

D/E	B/C
• some extended supported comments • unstructured response which tends to paraphrase • some identification of main points of argument • some awareness of methods of developing the argument.	• clear attempt to engage with the task • structured response • selects main points of argument and comments • a range of methods used to develop the argument.

The very brief student answer to Activity 4 falls into the D/E band but with more detail, more specific points and more on the methods that the author uses, it could easily have been in the B/C band.

Activity 5

You can now measure your own answer to Activity 4 against the mark scheme above. How do you think the student response compares to yours?

If you weren't able to write more than the student who wrote the example on page 33, then you need quite a lot of practice in writing these 10-minute answers. In the exam you are likely to be asked to write answers to four or five questions, so if you can practise using 10-minute writing sessions efficiently, then you will be preparing yourself very well for the exam.

What have I learnt?

Check that you:
- can find main points
- can omit examples and repetition that appear in the text
- can comment on the methods used to present or develop an argument
- know what the examiners are looking for
- can use the mark scheme descriptors to help you make sure that you can produce work in the B/C grade band.

In the future you:
- can practise this skill on your own with any pieces of writing you come across (you will encounter texts with an argument in many of your GCSE subjects – in textbooks and handouts).

5 Implications and inconsistencies

My learning

This chapter will help you to:
- identify implications
- identify inconsistencies
- improve your written response.

Assessment Objective

- Identify implications and recognise inconsistencies.

What you are being asked to do

This Assessment Objective can be tested on Paper 1. It won't be tested on Paper 2. However, in order to understand the Different Culture poems, tested in Paper 2, you need to be able to look at the implications of words and phrases in the poems. Therefore, it is helpful to think about this Assessment Objective for Paper 2 as well as for Paper 1.

Getting started

To show you know how to identify implications and inconsistencies, make sure you know that:
- an implication is something suggested or hinted at rather than directly stated
- you need to read between the lines
- implications may reveal attitudes or bias
- an inconsistency is where things don't really fit together
- an inconsistency is where there might be a contradiction.

> **Examiner hint**
>
> If you are asked to write about implications, words like 'suggests', 'implies' and 'could be the case' are useful.

Activity 1

Read the following example of a very short text where there is a puzzling inconsistency. The text came at the end of a form that had to be returned to the sender after completion. It is the part of the form where the return address could be seen through the window of the envelope that the form originally came in.

What is the inconsistency in the text?

Today's Cars (Magazine)

No stamp or envelope is required.

return to:

**Classic Cars Monthly
194 Birmingham Road
Coventry
CV12 8MG**

Insert in the envelope making sure that the address shown opposite can be viewed in the window.

**TELEPHONE HELPLINE:
01565 482976**

The text on page 37 is a 'leader' article from a newspaper. A leader is printed on the editorial page and gives the views of the newspaper on a topical issue. This one refers to an article elsewhere in the paper but, without it, the reader finds it very hard to understand. It also makes a lot of assumptions about what the reader knows, as well as implying things without stating them directly.

Read the text, then complete Activity 2.

Activity 2

1   Make a list of the different things the reader needs to know about in order to understand the newspaper article.
2   What is its attitude to the following:
  • Britain signing the EU Constitution   • Europe
  • Gordon Brown   • EU judges?

Now write a 10-minute answer to the following question:

How does The Sun *present its views about Britain signing the EU Constitution in this article? Point out any implications and inconsistencies you can find.*

No defence

THE 'impregnable' Maginot Line was intended to stop Hitler's army invading France in World War II.

In the end, German tanks simply drove round it and were on the streets of Paris in weeks.

Tory William Hague warns Britain's so-called defences against a federal Europe are just as flimsy.

Gordon Brown may draw as many 'red lines' as he likes. But as his own Labour MPs warned this week, they are built on sand.

EU judges will get round them with ease.

If the PM signs the EU Constitution in Lisbon this week, Britain will end up a puppet state.

With Brussels pulling all the strings.

From *The Sun*, 17 October 2007

What the examiners are looking for

The following is the kind of mark scheme an examiner might have if this were a question set in the exam. Read the mark scheme, then complete Activity 3 on page 38.

D/E	B/C
• some extended supported comment • unstructured response that tends to paraphrase • some identification of methods of presenting views • some comment on implications.	• clear and effective attempt to engage with task • structured response • selects and comments on methods of presentation • identifies and comments on implications and inconsistencies.

Activity 3

1   Read the following student's response to the same task. Then read
    the examiner comments around the article. As you read the student's
    response, try to keep the bullet points from the mark scheme on page 37
    in your mind. From this you should be able to work out your answer to
    the following question:

    Is the student's response in the D/E or B/C grade band? Why?

Implication

Implication

Supported point

Methods identified

Two implications

Supported point

Inconsistency
identified

Extended
supported
comment

> The Sun doesn't seem to like Europe or the
> EU because it says 'With Brussels pulling all
> the strings' in bold letters, underlined, at the
> end. It seems to prefer William Hague to
> Gordon Brown because it says Gordon Brown's
> ideas are 'built on sand'. It's hard to know
> what the reference to the Maginot Line is or
> why The Sun refers to it and to Hitler's army.
> It doesn't seem to have anything to do with
> signing the EU constitution.

2   Now, using the mark scheme on page 37, annotate your own answer
    to Activity 2, question 2. This will help you to check which of the mark
    scheme bullet points you have achieved and which grade band your
    answer falls into.

Another way that inconsistencies and implications might be
used is to amuse – for comic effect.

Read the newspaper article opposite, then complete Activity
4 on page 40.

The fantastic Mr Fly

BY ROSS McGUINNESS

A NEW musical talent has spread his wings and is already generating quite a bit of a buzz.

Meet Mr Fly, a piano-playing, guitar-bashing, musical genius from the insect world.

When he's not on stage or throwing up over his own food, he enjoys skateboarding, cycling and flying his kite.

Mr Fly is the unlikely muse of Belgian amateur photographer Nicholas Hendrickx.

Like his near namesake Jimi, the 21-year-old has torn up the rule book in his chosen field.

Nearly all the photographs of Mr Fly, whose first name is Gerald, were taken in Mr Hendrickx's bedroom, using mostly natural light and a small eight megapixel camera.

'I met Gerald Fly in my garden as I was shooting some flowers,' Mr Hendrickx said. 'There he was, staring at me with his big mosaic eyes, begging me for help. I offered him a job as my new model. That night we had a good drink and talked about potential photo shoots.'

'Surprisingly, he proved himself a lovely pianist and guitar player.'

In reality, Gerald is one of a number of flies which Mr Hendrickx photographs using props. 'It took quite some time. Some flies were great to work with, while others were very frustrating.'

Multi-talented: Mr Fly, (above), shows off in a skate park before tinkling the ivories and finally relaxing (below)

'I guess it's normal – flies and humans aren't made to work together. Flies are made to annoy us with their buzzing and pooping on stuff.' In explaining why he chose to put flies in front of the camera, Mr Hendrickx said: 'I guess I just wanted people to enjoy the little things in life and to give them a refreshing view on insect macro-photography.' He insists most of the shots feature live specimens, but how he gets a bug to read the paper on a deckchair is anyone's guess.

As for Gerald, he is reportedly seeking fame with his band The Buzzes, winging it through (very) small venues throughout Europe.

From *The Metro*, 5 November 2007

Activity 4

1   The writer implies that the fly is a star and a celebrity. Make a list of the ways he does this.

2   Make a list of the things that are impossible in reality in the article.

3   Write a 10-minute answer explaining how Ross McGuinness makes his article amusing.

What have I learnt?

Check that you:

- can find implications in what is written
- can identify and comment on any inconsistencies
- can use the mark scheme descriptors to help you make sure that your work is in the B/C grade band.

In the future you:

- can practise this skill on your own with any pieces of writing you come across
- will find inconsistencies in some pieces of writing
- will recognise that many texts have implications.

6 Select and make cross-references

What you are being asked to do

This Assessment Objective is tested a lot in the exam. You won't be asked a question that deals only with this Objective, but it is tested in both Paper 1 Section A and Paper 2 Section A every time you answer a question.

The Objective falls into three parts.
1 Select material appropriate to purpose.
2 Collate material from different sources.
3 Make cross-references.

Select material appropriate to purpose

This means:
- 'Answer the question'!
- Select details from the texts that support the points you make. Don't just describe what the text is about. Make sure that you think about the question and find material that fits it. This is especially true when you are writing an answer on the Poems from Different Cultures.

The recipe for success is to look very carefully at the key words of the task. Let's take an example.

Three things are tested in all the questions on Poetry from Different Cultures:
1 compare
2 poets' methods
3 knowledge, understanding and response to a topic.

A recent exam paper set the following question. Read the question and the notes around it, which explain what you are being asked to do.

How does Sujata Bhatt show that identity is important in '*from* Search For My Tongue'? Compare the methods she uses with the methods another poet uses to show that identity is important in one other poem.

'How' is asking for methods

The topic is 'identity is important'

Compare

You are asked to compare the methods

This is the topic

Activity 1

Using what you have just read above, find the key words in the task in each of the following questions.

a   Compare the methods used by John Agard in 'Half-Caste' with the methods used by another poet to present strong feelings.

b   Compare the methods the poets use to show what it is like to move from one country to another in 'Island Man' and 'Hurricane Hits England'.

c   Compare the ways Tom Leonard and John Agard use non-standard English in 'from Unrelated Incidents' and 'Half-Caste'.

d   Compare the ways people are presented in 'Night of the Scorpion' and 'Vultures'.

Now let's take an example of selecting material appropriate to purpose from Section A in Paper 1. The examiners have asked a question like this more than once. Read the question and the notes around it.

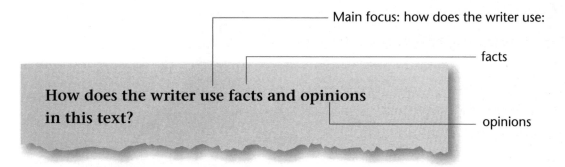

Main focus: how does the writer use:

facts

How does the writer use facts and opinions in this text?

opinions

To answer this question fully you need to:
- identify specific facts
- identify specific opinions
- comment on the use of each fact you choose
- comment on the use of each opinion you choose.

Advice from the examiner

1 Students who get a D often search for facts and for opinions and write down some examples of these in their answer. That is part of it, because unless you identify the facts and identify the opinions you can't say what you think their uses are. But the question itself asks for the central focus to be on 'uses'.

2 Given that you have about 10 minutes to answer this question, three or four facts and three or four opinions with a comment about the use of each one would make for a good answer.

3 The facts and opinions may not be used in the same way each time, so you will end up with an answer that considers several different uses. These might be: to inform; to persuade; facts used to support opinions; opinions used to agree with or contradict facts; to sustain or develop an argument, etc.

4 Of course, thinking carefully about the question takes some time and composure, and you will have the pressure of being in an exam. That is all the more reason not to rush into things but to spend some time thinking and then selecting appropriate material before you begin to write.

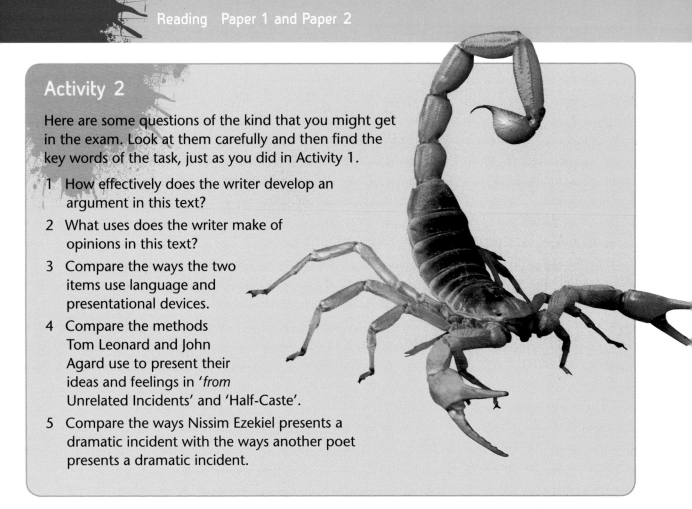

Activity 2

Here are some questions of the kind that you might get in the exam. Look at them carefully and then find the key words of the task, just as you did in Activity 1.

1 How effectively does the writer develop an argument in this text?

2 What uses does the writer make of opinions in this text?

3 Compare the ways the two items use language and presentational devices.

4 Compare the methods Tom Leonard and John Agard use to present their ideas and feelings in '*from* Unrelated Incidents' and 'Half-Caste'.

5 Compare the ways Nissim Ezekiel presents a dramatic incident with the ways another poet presents a dramatic incident.

Collate material from different sources

This part of the Assessment Objective refers mainly to the coursework you have done when you have looked at a range of texts and then chosen what material to write on.

'Collate' means 'put together'. In the exam you will be asked to put texts together by comparing them. On Paper 1 the question is likely to tell you which texts to compare. On Paper 2 each question names at least one poem, so you may have to choose the second poem yourself.

When answering your exam question on the Poems from Different Cultures, you should try to make a wise choice of your other poem! Look carefully at the question and think about which poem will go best with the named one for your purposes. And don't just choose on the basis of subject matter. You know that the question will ask you about how something or other is presented, so your wisest choice might be to think about similarities and differences in methods of presentation as well as similarities and differences in subject matter.

Activity 3

Here are some exam-style questions. Using your Anthology, focusing on **either** Cluster 1 **or** Cluster 2, complete the following for each of the four questions.

a Decide which poem you think would be the best to choose to go with the named poem.

b Decide what material you would select to answer the question, once you have chosen the second poem.

Note: In order to complete this activity in full, you will need to have studied all the poems in either Cluster 1 or Cluster 2. If you have not done this, choose only the questions for the poems that you have studied. You may have studied some poems from both clusters. If so, choose only the questions on the poems you have studied.

When it comes to choosing a second poem it doesn't matter whether it's from the same cluster or from the other one. The important thing is that it fits your purpose of answering the question fully and effectively.

Cluster 1

1 Compare the effects created by the poets' choice of structure in 'Limbo' and **one** other poem of your choice.

2 Compare the methods the poets use to present a dramatic event in 'Blessing' and **one** other poem of your choice.

3 Compare the methods the poets use to present a political message in 'Nothing's Changed' and **one** other poem of your choice.

4 Compare the ways people are presented in 'Two Scavengers in a Truck, Two Beautiful People in a Mercedes' and **one** other poem of your choice.

Cluster 2

5 Compare the ways description is used in 'This Room' and **one** other poem of your choice.

6 Compare the ways the experience of moving to another country is presented in 'Hurricane Hits England' and **one** other poem of your choice.

7 Compare the methods the poets use to create a lively speaking voice in 'from Unrelated Incidents' and **one** other poem of your choice.

8 Compare the methods the poets use to present feelings in 'Not My Business' and **one** other poem of your choice.

Make cross-references

This quite simply means 'Compare'. If you are also doing English Literature you will be used to comparing, because you have to compare in that exam when you are writing about poetry and if you are studying the short stories.

One of the questions in Section A of Paper 1 is very likely to ask you to compare, and all the Different Cultures poetry questions will ask you to compare.

'Compare' means:
* find similarities
* find differences
* find similarities within differences
* find differences within similarities.

Read the following attempts at comparison, written by students A, B and C. Then read what the examiner thought of these attempts.

Student A

> Sujata Bhatt and Moniza Alvi both use strong words. Sujata Bhatt says that her mother tongue would 'rot and die' whereas Moniza Alvi talks about her bangles which 'snapped, drew blood'.

What did the examiner think?

Student A's answer is vague and generalised. 'Strong words' is very general. It is not clear why the quoted words are 'strong'.

Student B

> Both 'This Room' and 'Blessing' use lists to create a sense of energetic activity but whereas the lists in 'This Room' are conventionally punctuated with commas, one of the lists in 'Blessing' (every man woman/child) has no commas in order to give a rapidly increasing sense of pace and urgency as the people rush out after the water from the burst pipe.

What did the examiner think?

Student B's answer is very precise and detailed.

Student C

> Both Edward Brathwaite and John Agard use repetition.

What did the examiner think?

Precise (but there is no detail or support).

Activity 4

Now decide if the following students' attempts at comparison are:

1 vague and generalised
2 precise
3 precise and detailed.

Student D

> The repetition of the slave chorus 'limbo/limbo like me' and of 'half' in 'Half-Caste' both show what the poets want to emphasise.

Student E

> Island Man doesn't like being in London. Neither does the person in 'Presents from my Aunts in Pakistan', an 'alien in the sitting room'.

Student F

> Both Ferlinghetti and Moniza Alvi scatter their lines over the page.

Student G

> The repetition in 'Island Man' ('groggily groggily' and 'muffling muffling') serves to highlight the subject's confused and perhaps sleepy state of mind, especially as the words run into each other because there are no commas, making the reader feel as uncertain as the character. Repetition in 'Half-Caste', though, has a very different effect. 'Half-Caste' is used six times in the first 30 short lines which makes the reader continue to think about whether 'half' is an appropriate word to use in any of these cases.

I'm sure you found that the more specific and the more detailed the comparisons are, the better they are. Practise making a precise comparison, developing it and showing what the effects of the writers' choices of presentation are.

What have I learnt?

Check that you:

- know how to answer the question
- can focus on the key words of the task
- can make precise, clear, detailed comparisons.

In the future:

- take time when you are given a question to work out exactly what it asks you to do
- practise writing some comparative sentences
- develop these sentences into a paragraph.

7 Language and its effects

My learning

This chapter will help you to:

- identify and comment on linguistic devices
- comment on the effects achieved by using them
- look at the ways language varies and changes according to context
- improve your response in the exam.

Assessment Objective

- Understand and evaluate how writers use linguistic devices to achieve their effects and comment on ways language varies and changes.

What you are being asked to do

You've been studying language since Key Stage 1 and you know a tremendous amount about it. You also looked at a lot of language features and their effects when studying the Poems from Different Cultures. It's important, when you are looking at the Paper 1 unseen non-fiction and media texts, and when you are looking at the Paper 2 Poems from Different Cultures, that you pay close attention to the language used and think about the effect it has on the reader.

Paper 1

Examiner hint

Keep adding to the list you have just made during the rest of the course. In this way you will have something useful to revise from and won't find your head going blank in the exam room.

Activity 1

1   Make a list of the different things you could write about if you were asked about language, such as adjective, metaphor and so on.

2   Compare your list with your partner or other members of your group and fill your lists out.

Activity 2

Read the extract below, then complete the following questions.

1 Make notes on the different kinds of language features Harold Nicolson uses to let the reader know how he is feeling.

2 For each of the things in your list you need to explain briefly how it shows his feelings.

18 October 1930

Feeling very depressed with life. Can't make out whether it is mere middle-aged depression or whether it is that I loathe journalism so much that it covers all my days with a dark cloud of shame. I feel that I have no time to add to my reputation by doing serious work and that my silly work day by day diminishes the reputation I have acquired ... In fact I feel a pretty feeble creature, just a soppy superficial humorist. I feel I would give my soul to leave the Standard but daren't because of the money. Middle-age for a hedonist like myself is distressing in any case, but with most people it coincides with an increase of power and income. [But] I have lost all serious employment, sacrificed my hopes, and am up against the anxiety of having not one penny beyond what I earn ... I have never been unhappy like this before.

From *The Independent*, 18 October 2007

Activity 3

Using the diary extract above, for each of the items in the following list, add a few words or phrases to show how these things bring out Nicolson's feelings. For example:

He repeats the words 'depressed' and 'depressing' because he wants the reader to take in how often he feels down.

Now add your 'because' to each of the following.

1 He begins with two minor sentences (sentences without main verbs).

2 He uses a metaphor ('dark cloud of shame').

3 He uses alliteration ('days ... dark').

4 He calls his work 'silly'.

5 He uses these words about himself: 'pretty feeble creature', 'soppy superficial'.

6 He uses a list of three ('lost all serious employment', 'sacrificed my hopes', 'up against ... anxiety').

7 He uses a conclusion.

8 There are many negatives ('dark cloud', 'distressing', 'not one penny').

In the exam, if you found five different things to say, gave an example of each and for each of them you made a specific comment on how his feelings were shown, then you would be getting a mark in the top band (A and A*). This is what you want to aim for. As it is, three comments, each with an example and comment, would probably put you in the C/B band.

But you need to make sure:

- each point is specific
- each point has an example
- each point has a comment.

Now look at the following answer from a student and the examiner comments around the text and at the end.

Word choice	Harold Nicholson says he is 'depressed'
Effect Language to support point	and shows the strength of his feelings by
	the emphatic word 'loathed'. He repeats
Language detail	'depressed'... 'depressing' because his depression
Writer's purpose	often happens. He shows how low he feels by
	piling on adjectives ('pretty feeble', 'soppy
Supported point with comment on effect	superficial') and makes the reader feel sorry
	for him and on his side by the colloquial,
Effect supported by two examples and two aspects of language	informal 'pretty feeble' and the contraction
	'don't'. His depression is shown by the metaphor
Effect, detail, language	'dark cloud of shame' and its extent by the use
Effect, detail, language	of the list of three in the last sentence.

What did the examiner think?

Although it's not particularly long, this answer includes eight different uses of language and supports each with a detail and comments on the effect of the language choice. It hasn't mentioned everything there is to say about language in the passage but it is full and detailed and gets an A.

Activity 4

1 Read the newspaper article below, then complete the following tasks.

Identify an example of each of the following language choices in the article and explain what its effect is.

a the language of the headline

b the language of the sub-heading

c the uses of slang

d the uses of adjectives

e the use of alliteration

f the appeals to different ages

g the uses of contemporary language

h the use of technical hairdressing jargon

i the uses of flattering language

j sentence length

k paragraph length.

FRINGE BENEFITS

FRINGES have never been so hot thanks to celebs such as Kate Moss, Cheryl Cole and *Strictly Come Dancing's* Gabby Logan.

The good news is they are versatile and an easy way to update your look with maximum effect and minimum effort.

Here, celebrity hairdresser **RICHARD WARD** gives his guide on how to make the look work for you.

Heavy, blunt fringes: Cheryl Cole, Kate Moss and Gabby Logan are all on-trend with their blunt, heavy fringes.

It works best with slim, oval faces and petite, delicate features and tends to make people look younger (think Christina Ricci).

As it is one of the boldest styles, you may need a wardrobe, hair colour and make-up revamp to carry it off.

This style should never sit above the eyebrows or it will look too schoolgirly, and requires precision cutting.

It is not the best on naturally very curly hair – fog, drizzle and damp

Latest look has maximum effect, minimum effort

weather will make your fringe shrink and frizz!

Soft, sweeping, side fringes: This look is great for older women as it is very face flattering. A soft, subtle fringe works brilliantly as a graduation between shorter layers and longer length (think Catherine Zeta Jones).

Great for most hair types, even curly, this fringe is low-maintenance and more forgiving. It can blend into the bulk of a haircut or can be more defined for extra versatility.

Layered, tapered fringes: Model of the moment, Agyness Deyn, wears her forward-sweeping, heavily layered fringe perfectly. This is a new, retro-inspired take on a traditional fringe. Hair needs to be expertly cut to look precise when worn groomed and sleek. This is great worn tousled and dishevelled too, and works best on hair with

natural movement without too much curl or frizz.

Fringe maintenance: This will depend on their style – blunt, heavy fringes need in-between trims, whereas softer looks require less grooming and can wait until haircut appointments.

Most good salons offer complimentary fringe trims between normal six to eight-week haircut appointments if necessary.

Golden Rules: Don't be tempted to trim fringes yourself – hairdressers take into account the amount hair stretches (up to one-third of its length when wet).

Face shape is paramount when considering a fringe – blunt, heavy fringes can make a face look rounder or squarer – so let your hairdresser be the judge of what works for you. Jaw-line, forehead length and face width should all be considered.

Fringes are a great way to disguise high foreheads and can make long faces look more uniform. Classic, slim oval faces carry off fringes the best.

From *The Sun*, 22 October 2007

2 Now write a 10-minute answer to this question:

How does the writer use language to make fringes seem desirable and attractive?

What the examiners are looking for

Read the following student's response to the same question.

The article makes fringes seem attractive by referring to attractive media women (Kate Moss, Cheryl Cole and Gabby Logan). It uses a lot of colloquial language ('shrink and frizz', 'make-up revamp', 'schoolgirly', 'retro-inspired') to appeal to the readers and make them think fringes are cool. It uses lots of positive and upbeat expressions to make fringes seem attractive, like 'very face-flattering' and 'a soft, subtle fringe works brilliantly'.

Here is the kind of mark scheme an examiner might have if this were a question set in the exam. This answer is in the D/E band – see if you can see why.

D/E

- some extended supported comment
- unstructured response and tends to paraphrase
- some identification of main features of language
- some awareness of the ways language is used.

B/C

- clear and effective attempt to engage with language use
- structured response
- selects and comments
- a range of examples
- identification of several features of language
- understanding of the uses of this language.

How can the answer be improved?

In order to be in the B/C band it needs to:

- make sure that all the points are about language (the first one isn't)
- make sure that the quotations always support the point ('schoolgirly' doesn't)
- make a wider range of points
- be more specific about language
- explain the points (the last one doesn't really show how the examples are 'positive')
- have more to say about the uses of language.

Activity 5

Swap your answer to question 2 in Activity 4 with a partner's. Mark each other's to see which of the mark scheme descriptors on page 54 you have achieved. Use the examiner's comments on page 52 to help you.

Activity 6

Now look at the uses of language in the two articles, on pages 51 and 53, together. They use different kinds of language because they:

- are different genres (diary and tabloid newspaper article)
- have different purposes (to explain the writer's depression and to persuade about fringes)
- are from different periods (1930 and 2007).

Jot down some of the differences between the two articles in:

- vocabulary
- sentence length
- sentence construction
- devices used
- purposes
- effects on the reader.

Paper 2

Exactly the same Assessment Objective is also tested on the Poems from Different Cultures in Paper 2. You are looking for the same things and also commenting on effect, just as you have done on the non-fiction and media texts.

Because you are likely to be studying just one cluster, go on to Activity 7 if you are studying Cluster 1 and Activity 8 if you are studying Cluster 2. If you are studying both clusters you could attempt both activities!

Activity 7 Cluster 1

1   Look at how Grace Nichols uses language in 'Island Man' to show how the Island Man is feeling. Make a list of the different kinds of language she uses.

2   Not only do you need to identify what devices are being used, but also you need to comment on their effect. You did this when you were writing about the fringes article in Activity 4.

So, looking at 'Island Man', jot down what you think the effect of each of the following is and how each shows his feelings:

a   one-word 'Morning' on its own line to open the poem (breaking the rules of grammar)

b   a transferred epithet 'wombing' applied to the surf but used to show how he feels (a transferred epithet is when a word relates to one thing but is applied to another)

c   lack of punctuation

d   sentences don't end with full stops in the 'right' places, with the result that they run into each other

e   alliteration of 'sun surfacing'

f   use of a precious jewel as an adjective to describe the island

g   repetition of 'groggily groggily' set off from the rest of the poem to the right-hand side

h   unexpected word 'soar'

i   sudden use of rhyming words ('soar' and 'roar')

j   another transferred epithet 'crumpled pillow waves', linking his sleepy state with the waves of the island

k   last line is one line on its own

l   no full stop at the end of the poem.

3   Now have a go at writing a 10-minute answer to this question:
How does Grace Nichols use language to show how Island Man is feeling?

....

Check your answer

Did you:
- manage to make several points
- support each point with specific detail
- make a comment about the effect of each of the things you wrote about?

If so then you are well on the way to achieving a C grade because you have 45 minutes in the exam to answer the question and although that will involve comparison between two poems, you still have a lot of time left to develop your points and to make a range of comparisons.

Activity 8 Cluster 2

1 Look at how Grace Nichols uses language in 'Hurricane Hits England' to show how she feels about the hurricane coming to England. Make a list of the different kinds of language she uses.

2 Not only do you need to identify what devices are being used but also you need to comment on their effect. You did this when you were writing about the fringes article in Activity 4.

So, looking at 'Hurricane Hits England', jot down what you think the effect of each of the following is and how each shows her feelings:

a poems starts in third person ('her', 'she')

b paradox (opposite meanings both true) of 'Fearful and reassuring'

c shift from third to first person ('her/she', 'me/I')

d lack of punctuation between the names of the three different gods (Huracan, Oya, Shango)

e two questions, perhaps rhetorical ones (do they expect an answer or not?)

f clever ambiguity of 'short-circuit us' which relates to how people experience the hurricane and also to the electricity cuts which accompany the hurricane

g dramatic simile of trees falling as heavy as whales

h link between land (of England) and sea (of Caribbean)

i sound patterns of 'heavy as whales'

j alliteration of 'crusted' and 'cratered'

k another rhetorical question

l repetition of 'I am' in the three parallel phrases

m emphatic 'Ah'

n ritual repetition of 'Come to' in the last stanza

o repetition in the last line

p very open meaning of the last line of the poem.

3 Now have a go at writing a 10-minute answer to this question:

How does Grace Nichols use language to show how she feels about the hurricane coming to England?

Check your answer

Did you:

• manage to make several points

• support each point with specific detail

• make a comment about the effect of each of the things you wrote about?

If so then you are well on the way to achieving a C grade because you have 45 minutes in the exam to answer the question and although that will involve comparison between two poems, you still have a lot of time left to develop your points and to make a range of comparisons.

There are plenty of practice tasks and examples for you to work on in Chapter 9: Poems from Different Cultures and Traditions (pages 69 to 90).

What have I learnt?

Check that you:

- can identify aspects of language and linguistic devices
- can comment on effect
- can see how language is used differently in different contexts and on different occasions
- know what the examiners are looking for
- can use the mark scheme descriptors to help you make sure that you produce work in the higher band.

In the future you:

- can practise this skill on your own with any pieces of writing you come across – for example, advertisements, articles, textbooks, newspapers, magazines and poems.

8 Structure and presentational devices

My learning

This chapter will help you to:

• identify and comment on presentational devices

• identify and comment on structural devices

• improve your responses in the exam.

Assessment Objective

• Understand and evaluate how writers use structural and presentational devices to achieve their effects.

This Assessment Objective is tested both on Paper 1 Section A and on Paper 2 Section A, so you will need to practise it on the non-fiction and media texts and on the Poems from Different Cultures.

Paper 1

Activity 1

1 Make two lists as follows.

   a The different things you could write about if you were asked about presentational devices in a text.

   b The different things you could write about if you were asked about structural devices in a text.

2 Compare your list with your partner or other members of your group and fill your lists out.

Examiner hint

Keep adding to your presentational and structural lists. This will give you something useful to revise from.

Look at the document on page 60, which is the last page of a booklet about Sir John Soane's Museum in London. Then complete Activity 2 on page 61.

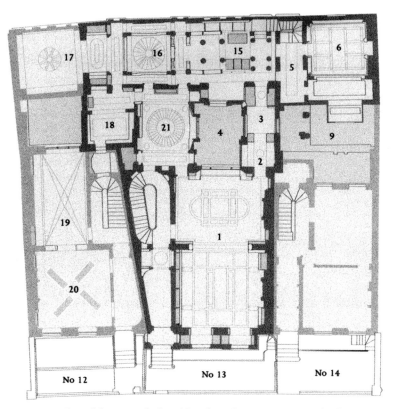

Plan of the Ground Floor (for Plan of Basement see overleaf)

Sir John Soane's Museum is open free: Tuesday to Saturday inclusive, 10am – 5pm. Also on the first Tuesday of each month, 6 – 9pm. Closed Sunday, Monday, Bank Holidays and Christmas Eve. Public lecture tour every Saturday at 11am, except as above. 22 tickets are available from 10.30am at a cost of £5 each, free to students.

Group visits to the Museum must be booked in advance and the group may be no more than 20 in number. Group visits may not be booked for Saturdays or for the first Tuesday of the month evening opening. Access to the Research Library and collections of manuscripts and architectural drawings is by appointment.

The Museum welcomes the support of individuals who can help in different ways. The Development Department organises a varied programme of lectures, private views, visits to private collections and social events for Soane Patrons and Soane Supporters. If you would like information on these groups or details of how it is possible to help the Museum, please contact Mike Nicholson on 0207 440 4241 or mnicholson@soane.org.uk

Sir John Soane's Museum   13 Lincoln's Inn Fields London WC2A 3BP
Tel: General Enquiries 020 7405 2107   Research Library: 020 7440 4251
Group bookings: 020 7440 4263 or email jbrock@soane.org.uk
Registered Charity No: 313609   Website: www.soane.org   Fax: 020 7831 3957

Plans drawn by Christopher Hawkesworth Woodward (1996). Designed by Libanus Press. Printed by Hampton Printing, Bristol. Revised January 2008

Activity 2

1 Look at this list of presentational and structural devices that are very often used and see how many of them you can find in the museum document on page 60:

Presentational devices:

- bold, italic, underlining
- headlines, sub-headings, pictures, graphics, charts, graphs, logos, website addresses, colour.

Structural devices:

- paragraphs, stanzas, bullet points, sections
- introduction, conclusion, summary, repetition, chorus
- discourse features such as 'firstly', 'secondly', 'in conclusion'.

2 For each of the examples you have found, say how effective you think it is in getting information across to the reader.

For example, you might start with:

The plan of the ground floor lets the reader see the layout of the house, so that you can walk round and know where you are.

Activity 3

Using the museum document on page 60, write a 10-minute answer to the following question:

How effective are the presentational and structural devices in getting information across and influencing the reader on this page?

Now read the newspaper article on the next page. Then complete Activity 4.

THE ELEPHANT MEN

3 in 5 Brit fellas will be obese by 2050

By EMMA MORTON, Health and Science Editor

THREE in five British men will be OBESE in 40 years' time – bringing the nation to a halt, a shock report reveals.

Many will be unable to work or even walk down the street.

And their chronic health problems like heart disease and diabetes will cost the health service **£45BILLION** a year by 2050.

The Department of Health document blamed the crisis on 'healthy behaviours being a challenge in today's society' – rather than Britons getting fatter through laziness.

It said modern life was geared towards helping adults **GAIN** weight, with fast food firms and modern technology named as the main culprits – and that the country needs an overhaul to stop us eating to death.

The figures come in the hard-hitting Foresight report by the Government's top doctors and scientists.

It warned that there was no wonder-drug cure. Instead, it called for changing transport systems in every city to get people walking more.

If they do not, being morbidly obese will become the norm.

The report also shows that half of women and a quarter of children will be obese by the middle of the century.

Cheap

Head of the Foresight programme, Sir David King, said: 'Personal responsibility is important but the problem is much more complicated'.

'With energy-dense, cheap foods, labour-saving devices, motorised transport and sedentary work, obesity is rapidly becoming a consequence of modern life.' Health groups said the report was a wake-up call.

Dr David Haslam, of the National Obesity Forum, said: 'The sobering thought that the super obese will die before they are 30 because of heart problems and diabetes should encourage people to make changes to their diet and lifestyle. This report provides a catalyst for change.'

Cancer research UK said around 12,000 people each year could avoid getting the disease if they stayed slim.

Spokeswoman Sara Hiom added: 'The evidence linking obesity to an increased risk of cancer is compelling.

'More effort is needed to ensure that an effective and fully integrated obesity prevention strategy is in place to help tackle the problem.'

e.morton@the-sun.co.uk

Normal size .. in near future

From *The Sun*, 17 October 2007

Activity 4

1 Make a list of all the structural and presentational devices you can find in 'The Elephant Men' newspaper article.

   Make sure that you are as precise and detailed as you can be. For instance, don't just say it has a picture; instead be precise about what you can see. And instead of saying that there is a headline, be precise about what the headline is like. The more precise and detailed your observations are, the easier it will be to say what you think the effect is.

2 For each of the things in your list above, jot down how effective it is in supporting the text and interesting the reader.

Check your answer

Looking back at your answers to Activity 4, how close was your observation? Did you mention:

- the way THE is printed on the headline – it's uneven, at an angle and partly imposed on the top of ELEPHANT
- that the sub-heading is white on a black background
- that the sub-heading is underlined in white
- that the black background to it has uneven wavy edges
- the use of numbers in the sub-heading
- that the man's black baseball cap merges with the sub-heading
- that the man's belly pushes into the print
- the different sizes of black capitals on the page
- the italics for what Cancer Research said and for the email address
- the one-word sub-heading in the middle of the article?

If you only made very general reference to some of these features, then it would be difficult to say much about their effect. When the observations are very detailed and precise, then you can make some precise and detailed comments about their effect.

Activity 5

Now write a 10-minute answer to the following question:

How effectively does 'The Elephant Man' article opposite use structural and presentational devices in getting information across and influencing the reader?

Here is an answer to this same question by a student. Read the student's answer together with the examiner's comments, which shows where the student gives evidence of the skills.

This article is about sixty per cent of British men being obese in forty years' time. The most important words on the page are picked out in capital letters. The shocking headline 'The Elephant Men' and the emphasis on 'OBESE' in the first paragraph get the message across to the reader clearly. The picture of the man with the enormous belly pushing its way into the page and pushing the print aside is an amusing but horrible image. The italics emphasise an important message from Cancer Research U.K. and the figures, as elsewhere in the article, drive the point home. The article is clearly structured, with the main point at the beginning, followed by the research and then some expert opinions. It's not at all clear to me why they picked out and underlined the sub-heading 'Cheap' half way through the article. 'Cheap' is not important to the article.

Marginal annotations (left):
- Presentation
- Comment on presentation (though general); influencing reader
- Presentation
- Presentation
- General comment on effect; influencing reader
- Comment on structure
- Details of structure
- Comment on presentation and structure; influencing reader

Marginal annotations (right):
- Presentation; influencing reader
- Presentation
- Clear comment on presentation and effect
- Presentation
- Structured response to task
- Extended and developed comment about structure
- Extended and developed comment

What did the examiner think?

The following is taken from the sort of mark scheme the examiner might use to mark this answer.

D/E	B/C
• some extended supported comment • unstructured response and tends to paraphrase • some identification of main structural features • some identification of main presentational devices • some comment on effect of structural and presentational devices.	• clear attempt to engage with task • structured response • selects and comments on effects of structural devices • selects and comments on effects of presentational devices • material clearly linked to getting information across and influencing the reader.

The student's answer on page 64 achieves all the B/C bullet points (descriptors).

Activity 6

Look closely at your own answer in Activity 5 to see which of the descriptors (the bullets in the mark scheme above) you have met.

If you have not met your targets in your own answer, rewrite it so that you do, bearing the mark scheme descriptors closely in mind.

Paper 2

Exactly the same skills are tested in Paper 2 on the Poems from Different Cultures as are tested on the non-fiction and media texts. It is the same Assessment Objective.

On the Poetry you will probably be studying either Cluster 1 or Cluster 2. If you are studying Cluster 1, do Activity 7. If you are studying Cluster 2 do Activity 8. If you are studying both clusters you could attempt both activities!

Activity 7 Cluster 1

1   Look at how Edward Kamau Brathwaite uses structural and presentational devices in 'Limbo'. Make a list of the different things that you can identify.

2   In the exam you need to be able to:

- identify which devices are being used
- comment on their effect.

Jot down what you think the **effect** of each of the following is and how they reflect the ideas in the poem:

a   starting the poem ungrammatically with 'And'

b   the capital A of 'And' being the only capital letter in the poem

c   the use of italics

d   the repetition of 'limbo/limbo like me' at frequent points in the poem

e   the rhyming words 'ready' and 'steady'

f   the repetitions throughout which are themselves repeated

g   one-word lines

h   groups of one line, two lines, three lines and four lines

i   the frequent gaps in the poem

j   the one piece of punctuation is a full stop at the end.

3   Now have a go at writing a 10-minute answer to this question:

How does Brathwaite use structural and presentational devices to present his ideas in 'Limbo'?

....

Check your answer

Did you:

- manage to make several points
- expand and develop your points
- comment on the effect of each of the things you chose to write about
- link each point you made with the ideas in the poem?

If so then you are well on the way to achieving a C grade because you have 45 minutes in the exam to answer the question and, although that will involve comparison between two poems, you still have a lot of time left to develop and link your points and to make a range of comparisons.

Activity 8 Cluster 2

1 Look at how Niyi Osundare uses structural and presentational devices in 'Not My Business'. Make a list of the different things that you can identify.

2 In the exam you need to be able to:
- identify what devices are being used
- comment on their effect.

Jot down what you think the **effect** of each of the following is and how they reflect the ideas in the poem:

a starting the poem with 'They' without explaining who 'they' are

b each line starting with a capital letter

c the indentation of the final three lines of each of the first three stanzas

d the last stanza having only five lines

e the last stanza lacking indentation

f the use of question marks

g the use of the colon

h the use of the dash

i the repetition of the last three lines in each of the first three stanzas

j the list of three in 'No query, no warning, no probe'

k the way 'Waiting, waiting' echoes the 'waiting' of the first stanza

l the balance, regularity and formal organisation of the poem.

3 Now have a go at writing a 10-minute answer to this question:

How does Osundare use structural and presentational devices to present his ideas in 'Not My Business'?

....

Check your answer

Did you:
- manage to make several points
- expand and develop your points
- comment on the effect of each of the things you chose to write about
- link each point you made with the ideas in the poem?

If so then you are well on the way to achieving a C grade because you have 45 minutes in the exam to answer the question and, although that will involve comparison between two poems, you still have a lot of time left to develop and link your points and to make a range of comparisons.

There are plenty of practice tasks and examples for you to work on in Chapter 9: Poems from Different Cultures (pages 69 to 90).

What have I learnt?

Check that you:

- know how to identify structural or presentational devices
- know how to comment on their effects
- know what the examiners are looking for
- can use the mark scheme descriptors to help you make sure that you produce work in the higher band.

In the future you:

- can practise this skill on your own with any pieces of writing you come across, such as newspaper articles, magazine articles, diagrams and poems.

9 Poems from Different Cultures and Traditions

My learning

This chapter will help you to:

- understand what the examiners are looking for
- revise key features of the poems
- prepare for this section of the exam
- improve your response.

Assessment Objectives

- Read with insight and engagement, making appropriate reference to texts and developing and sustaining interpretations of them.
- Select material appropriate to purpose, collate material from different sources, and make cross-references.
- Understand and evaluate how writers use linguistic, structural and presentational devices to achieve their effects, and comment on ways language varies and changes.

What you are being asked to do

It is likely that you will be studying only one of the two clusters of poems. In the exam, Question 1 will be based on Cluster 1 and Question 2 will be based on Cluster 2. You don't have to have studied all the poems in both clusters but you need to have prepared all the poems in one cluster. This is because each question must name one poem.

When you are comparing the named poem with another, you can choose this other poem from either cluster if you happen to have prepared more poems than are in your main cluster.

The following are the mark schemes that the examiner uses to mark these exam questions.

Notional D

- awareness of feeling(s), attitude(s), idea(s)
- range of comment supported by textual details with some valid cross-reference
- comment on effects achieved by writer.

Notional C

- understanding of feelings, attitudes, ideas
- range of extended supported comment with some developed cross-reference
- awareness of writers' techniques and purpose.

Notional B

- appreciation of feelings, attitudes and ideas
- effective use of textual detail with integrated cross-reference
- understanding of a variety of writers' techniques and purposes.

In the exam the question will ask you to do three things because every question has to test the Assessment Objectives. Every question will ask you to:

- write about a topic
- comment on the writers' choices and their effects
- compare.

In order to move up from a D to a C you need to be able to:

- answer the question very precisely
- write about four or five different methods that the poet has chosen
- make some precise comparisons of these methods
- write about the effects of the writers' choices.

These are all skills that you can practise.

Here are some examples of these skills in action. They are not, of course, whole answers and in the exam the examiner will be looking for you to show each of these skills at some stage in your answer.

Read student responses A and B on page 71 and the comments from the examiner (which use the mark scheme descriptors).

Student A

Method

Aware of feelings

Supported comment

Extended comment on the way towards effect

> The speaker in 'Night of the Scorpion' shows that he doesn't like the neighbours coming in. They are like insects ('like swarms of flies') and 'Buzzed' the name God, perhaps like a wasp.

Student B

> The speaker reveals complex and mixed feelings about the neighbours in 'Night of the Scorpion'. Although they are described as insects ('like swarms of flies'; 'buzzed the name of God') and made irritating noises ('clicked their tongues'), they are nevertheless shown as caring for his mother ('they sat around/ on the floor with my mother in the centre') and are using their religious beliefs and rituals to try to help her ('the peace of understanding on each face'; the prayers they say). The sounds help the reader to understand the chaos and bustle in the room by imagining they are hearing it.

Method

Understanding of attitudes

Supported comment

Extended supported comment

Effective use of textual detail

Explanation of effect

Activity 1

Now see if you can create annotations for the following extracts from student answers using the mark scheme skills descriptors on page 70:

Student C

Painting and music are obvious ways of showing that mixing black and white does not lead to half of anything. Agard's reference to the weather, however, making a joke about English weather to his (presumably) English audience lightens the tone of the poem. Even if the other sections of the poem can be read in an angry tone, the joke about the weather and the rather crude mention of the sun passing 'ah rass' draws the reader in rather than setting him or her aside. This technique of getting the audience on his side is directly opposed by Leonard's confrontational tactics, calling the reader 'wanna yoo scruff' and telling him or her to 'belt up' at the end.

Student D

The inclusion of the Gujerati in 'from Search For My Tongue', makes the reader know what it feels like to be confronted by a foreign language, seeing a strange script and not being even able to pronounce it.

If you are studying only Cluster 1 then work through pages 73 to 82. If you are only studying Cluster 2, work through pages 82 to 90. If you are studying both clusters, you could work through both of the following sections!

Cluster 1

My Learning

This section will help you to:

- focus on feelings, attitudes and ideas
- focus on writers' methods of presentation
- focus on comparison
- improve your written response.

Feelings, attitudes and ideas

A typical question on Cluster 1 might be:

Compare the ways people are presented in 'Two Scavengers in a Truck, Two Beautiful People in a Mercedes' and 'Island Man'.

Activity 2

Looking at the two poems 'Two Scavengers in a Truck, Two Beautiful People in a Mercedes' and 'Island Man', either discuss or jot down answers to the following questions.

1 What are the people like in 'Two Scavengers in a Truck, Two Beautiful People in a Mercedes'?
2 Find some similarities and differences between the garbage men and the beautiful people.
3 What links does Ferlinghetti find between them?
4 Why do you think the writer chooses to have them stop together at the traffic lights?
5 What is Island Man like in Grace Nichols's poem?
6 Where is he and what does he feel?
7 How does Grace Nichols show you how he feels?

Finally,

8 Using your answers from questions 1–7, write one or two paragraphs on the following topic. You need to show that you have understood the feelings, attitudes and ideas in the poems.

Compare the ways people are presented in 'Two Scavengers …' and 'Island Man'.

Activity 3

Have a go at writing one paragraph on each of the following questions.

Remember when you are writing that you are concentrating on showing that you understand feelings, attitudes and ideas in the poems.

1 Compare the ways feelings are presented in 'Limbo' and 'Nothing's Changed'.

2 Compare the ways a dramatic event is presented in 'Blessing' and 'Night of the Scorpion'.

3 Compare the methods used to present people's attitudes to a terrible event in 'Vultures' and 'What Were They Like?'.

Writers' methods of presentation

Another typical question on Cluster 1 might be:

Compare the methods Imtiaz Dharker and Nissim Ezekiel use to present a dramatic event in 'Blessing' and 'Night of the Scorpion'.

Activity 4

Looking at the two poems 'Blessing' and 'Night of the Scorpion', either discuss or jot down answers to the following questions.

1 Identify the lists in 'Blessing'.

2 Are they all punctuated in the same way?

3 Identify the repeated 's' sounds in the poem.

4 Why do you think Imtiaz Dharker includes so many of these?

5 Identify some uses of alliteration.

6 What effects are created by these?

7 Identify the repetitions in 'Night of the Scorpion'.

8 What effects do these create?

9 Find the sentences that don't have main verbs in them (these are called minor sentences).

10 Why do you think Ezekiel has written them like this?

11 Find some uses of alliteration.

12 What effects are created by these?

Finally,

13 Using your answers from questions 1–12, write one paragraph on the following topic. Show that you have understood the writers' methods of presentation, the effects they have created and their purposes in writing in the ways they have done.

Compare the methods Imtiaz Dharker and Nissim Ezekiel use to present a dramatic event in 'Blessing' and 'Night of the Scorpion'.

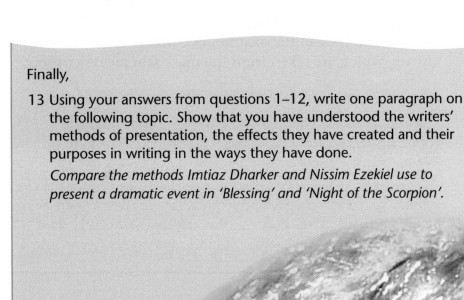

Now read the following student response to the same question. Then read the examiner's comments around the answer, which are taken from the mark scheme descriptors.

Comment on effect ——————

Aware of writer's purpose ——————

Aware of writer's technique ——————

Comment on effect ——————

Clear awareness of purpose ——————

> Both writers use alliteration in their poems to make the reader take notice of what they are saying. Imtiaz Dharker writes of a 'small splash' which makes the reader hear the water and then at the end of the poem she links the water with the children by 'sings' and 'small' and by 'blessing' and 'bones'. Ezekiel emphasises the main topic of the poem right at the beginning by the alliteration of 'stung by a scorpion' and at the end of the poem he makes you visualise the father lighting the mother's toe by 'flame feeding'. Because the reader visualises this it makes you realise the horror of what she is going through.

Notional D	Notional C	Notional B
• comments on effects achieved by writer.	• awareness of writers' techniques and purposes.	• understanding of a variety of writers' techniques.

Activity 5

1   Compare your own answer with the one above, trying to match yours to the mark scheme descriptors. Is your answer better or worse than the answer above?

To help you, to improve their answer this student needs to:

- be more precise about the comparisons
- be more precise about the effects on the reader
- write about more techniques (she only writes about one although she just about manages to identify two effects)
- use all the material she found in the answers she gave to Activity 4, questions 1–12
- link her material to the writers' purposes.

2   Rewrite your own answer if you have not already achieved a C or B.

Activity 6

Have a go at writing one paragraph on each of the following questions.

Remember when you are writing your paragraph that you are concentrating on showing that you understand the writers' methods of presentation, the effects created and the writers' purposes.

1 Compare the ways the writers use sounds and repetition in 'Limbo' and 'Blessing'.

2 Compare the methods the writers use to present the ways the speakers feel in 'Night of the Scorpion' and 'Nothing's Changed'.

3 Compare the effects created by the layout of the poems in 'What Were They Like?' and 'Limbo'.

Use of textual detail and comparison

Another typical question on Cluster 1 might be:

Compare the methods the poets use to present their ideas in 'Nothing's Changed' and 'Vultures'.

Activity 7

Looking at the two poems 'Nothing's Changed' and 'Vultures', either discuss or jot down answers to the following questions.

1 Why do you think 'Nothing's Changed' begins with the description of grasses and weeds?

2 Look at how the poem is structured with 'No board says it is' paralleled by 'No sign says it is' and with stanzas 5 and 6 contrasting the restaurants.

3 Picks out the words that suggest violence.

4 What effect does this have on the reader?

5 What words and phrases suggest what the speaker of the poem feels?

6 What different things do you think are meant by 'Nothing's changed'?

7 In what ways are the vultures and the commandant similar in 'Vultures'?

8 In what ways are they different?

9 What do you think the poet means in the last four lines of the poem?

10 Identify some parts of the poem written in non-standard grammar and say what you think the effect of this is.

11 Pick out phrases describing something unpleasant.

12 Look at the structure of the poem. What is the main point being made in each of the four stanzas?

Finally,

13 Using your answers from Activity 7, write one paragraph on the following topic. Concentrate on making comparisons and supporting these with textual detail.

Compare the methods the poets use to present their ideas in 'Nothing's Changed' and 'Vultures'.

Activity 8

1   Now use the mark scheme descriptors to decide on the level of skills
    you are achieving in your answer to question 13 in Activity 7.

Notional D	**Notional C**	**Notional B**
• range of comment supported by textual details with some valid cross-reference.	• range of extended supported comment with some developed cross-reference.	• effective use of textual detail with integrated cross-reference.

2   Rewrite your answer if you have not achieved a C or a B.

Activity 9

Have a go at writing one paragraph on each of the following questions.

Remember when you are writing your paragraph that you are concentrating on using textual details effectively and making a range of developed comparisons.

1   Compare the effects created by the choices of structure made by Afrika and Brathwaite in 'Nothing's Changed' and 'Limbo'.

2   Compare the methods used to present people in 'Island Man' and 'Blessing'.

3   Compare the methods the poets use to present disturbing events in 'Vultures' and 'What Were They Like?'

The Assessment Objective as a whole

Now that you have looked at each of the skills in turn, it is time to put them all together.

Let's find out what you already know about 'Limbo' and 'What Were They Like?'.

Activity 10

1   Looking at the two poems 'Limbo' and 'What Were They Like?', either jot down or discuss answers to the following questions.

   a   What do you think each poem is about?

   b   What do you learn about the point of view of the voice of the poem during the course of it?

   c   What methods do the poets use to present these ideas and points of view?

2 Now discuss or jot down what you can say about:

    a how the kinds of oppression in the poems are similar and/or different

    b what the poets have to say about oppression

    c the methods they use to do it.

3 Now write your answer in full to the following question:

Compare the methods the poets use to present oppression in 'Limbo' and 'What Were They Like?'

Examiner hints

- You don't have to have lots of comparisons. About three will be enough. Then you can fill them out and develop them as you are writing your essay.
- Make sure that you remember the three different things the examiners are looking for:
  - response to feelings, attitudes and ideas
  - the poets' methods of presentation and the effect of these on the reader
  - detailed textual reference and comparison.
- Aim to write about five paragraphs.

Remind yourself of the mark scheme descriptors which the examiners will be using.

Notional D	Notional C	Notional B
• awareness of feeling(s), attitude(s), idea(s) • range of comments supported by textual details with some valid cross-reference • comment on effects achieved by writers.	• understanding of feelings, attitudes, ideas • range of extended supported comment with some developed cross-reference • awareness of writers' techniques and purposes.	• appreciation of feelings, attitudes, ideas • effective use of textual detail with integrated cross-reference • understanding of a variety of writers' techniques and purposes.

Look at the extract below, taken from a student's response to the same question you attempted in question 3 of Activity 10. Look at the annotations to see how the mark scheme descriptors have been applied by the examiner.

Method
Method
Method
Extended comment

Effect

Effect
Valid cross-reference

Effect

I think 'Limbo' says a lot about oppression because Brathwaite is writing in the persona of a person on a slave ship, giving a series of snapshot moments with a chorus perhaps of what the slaves are singing. The overall impression is of darkness and slavery and violence ('stick is the whip', 'the dark deck is slavery'). Although he does not state it directly, there are suggestions of rape ('knees spread wide and the dark ground is under me'). The repetition of 'knees spread wide' makes the reader stop and think about what this could possibly mean. There is also a sense that time moves slowly by lots of parts of the poem having very short sections with only one word on a line.

The oppression in 'What Were They Like?' is of an even more violent kind. The poem starts with six numbered questions about what the people of Vietnam were like before the Vietnam war. This is a very unusual way to write a poem; it seems at first to be more like a quiz. The second section of the poem consists of some answers which relate to the questions asked first. What sounds attractive and perhaps romantic ('reverence the opening of buds') in the first section turns to horror in the second section as we realise the children were killed. Levertov uses a metaphor for this. The buds become the children. Because she has chosen 'buds' it makes us think that what is natural has been destroyed.

Both poets present oppression. The oppression in 'Limbo' is from the point of view of a slave on a slave ship, but 'What Were They Like?' is in the form of a question and answer session. The answers seem to come from someone of an inferior rank because two of them start with 'Sir'.

Understanding of technique and effect

Valid cross-reference

What did the examiner think?

The student's answer above is notionally a Grade D answer, although there are some parts of it which suggest a C.

To be secure in C the student needs to:
- be more precise in the comparisons
- make more comparisons, rather than dealing with the poems separately
- write more about the effects of the writers' choices
- be more accurate and precise about the similarities and differences between the poets' methods of presenting oppression
- comment on the writers' purposes.

To get a notional B the student needs to:
- examine a range of comparisons, based on the poets' methods
- show appreciation of a range of the writers' techniques of presentation
- develop an argument through the essay
- make sure that the examples, details and comparisons are integrated with the argument
- show understanding of the writers' purposes.

Activity 11

If you haven't already achieved a C or a B, rewrite your own answer to question 3 of Activity 10.

What have I learnt?

Check that you:

• know how to answer the poetry questions
• know what the examiners are looking for.

In the future you:

• can practise these skills either individually or together on any pair of poems
• could do this once a day or even once every two days between now and the exam; you would know the poems really well and be very well prepared for the exam.

Cluster 2

My learning

This section will help you to:

• focus on feelings, attitudes and ideas
• focus on writers' methods of presentation
• focus on comparison
• improve your written response.

Feelings, attitudes and ideas

A typical question on Cluster 2 might be:

Compare the ways poets present their ideas and feelings in 'from Search For My Tongue' and 'Love After Love'.

Activity 12

Looking at the two poems 'from Search For My Tongue' and 'Love After Love', either discuss or jot down answers to the following questions.

1   What does Sujata Bhatt say about language in 'from Search For My Tongue?'

2   How does she extend and develop the metaphor of her tongue as a plant?

3   What are her feelings at the end of the poem when she says that her tongue 'blossoms out of my mouth'?

4   Why do you think she includes the Gujerati script and the English transcription of it?

5   How does Derek Walcott use the image of the mirror in 'Love After Love'?

6   How do you think the speaker of the poem feels at the end of the poem? What evidence can you find for what you think?

7   What story is Walcott alluding to in his references to 'Eat', 'Give wine. Give bread'? Why do you think he says this?

8   How precise and clear is Derek Walcott in what his poem is about?

Finally,

9   Using your answers from questions 1–8, write one paragraph on the following topic, showing that you have understood the ideas, attitudes and feelings in the poem:

Compare the ways poets present their ideas and feelings in 'from *Search For My Tongue' and 'Love After Love'.*

Activity 13

Have a go at writing one paragraph on each of the following questions.

Remember when you are writing your paragraph that you are concentrating on showing that you understand feelings, attitudes and ideas in the poems.

1   Compare the ways feelings are presented in 'from Unrelated Incidents' and 'Half-Caste'.

2   Compare the ways a dramatic event is presented in 'This Room' and 'Not My Business'.

3   Compare the methods used to present people's attitudes to moving from one country to another in 'Hurricane Hits England' and 'Presents from my Aunts in Pakistan'.

Writers' methods of presentation

Another typical question on Cluster 2 might be:

Compare the methods Imtiaz Dharker and Niyi Osundare use to present a dramatic event in 'This Room' and 'Not My Business'.

Activity 14

Looking at the two poems 'This Room' and 'Not My Business', either discuss or jot down answers to the following questions.

1 Identify the lists in 'This Room'.
2 Identify the repeated hard sounds in the poem.
3 Why do you think Imtiaz Dharker includes so many of these?
4 Identify some uses of alliteration.
5 What effects are created by these?
6 Identify the repetitions in 'Not My Business'.
7 What effects do these create?
8 Look at the violent words in 'Not My Business'.
9 Why do you think Osundare has included them?
10 Find some uses of alliteration.
11 What effects are created by these?
12 Find two examples of personification.
13 What effect is created by the use of these?

Finally,

14 Using your answers from questions 1–13, write one paragraph on the following topic. Show that you have understood the writers' methods of presentation, the effects they have created and their purposes in writing in the ways they have done.

Compare the methods Imtiaz Dharker and Niyi Osundare use to present a dramatic event in 'This Room' and 'Not My Business'.

Now read the student's response to the same question below, together with the examiner's comments, taken from the mark scheme descriptors.

Imtiaz Dharker writes about the event of her ceiling falling down and everything going topsy turvey in the present tense, while Niyi Osundare tells a story of political threat using the past tense. Imtiaz Dharker makes the reader feel the increasing speed of events by using lists culminating in the quickly moving 'fly by the ceiling fan', while Osundare uses a chorus to show the inevitability that in the end someone will come for him.

— Method

— Method

— Method and effect

Notional D	Notional C	Notional B
• comments on effects achieved by writer.	• awareness of writers' techniques and purposes.	• understanding of a variety of writers' techniques.

Activity 15

1 Compare your own answer with the student's answer above, trying to match them both up with the mark scheme descriptors. Is your answer better or worse than the student's?

To improve the answer this student needs to:

- be more precise about the comparisons
- be more precise about the effects on the reader
- use a lot more detail
- write about more techniques (she only writes about two and has very little to say about the second one)
- use all the material she found in the answers she gave when she completed Activity 14, questions 1–13
- link her material to the writers' purposes.

2 Rewrite your own answer if you have not already achieved a C or B.

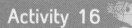

Activity 16

Have a go at writing one paragraph on each of the following questions.

Remember when you are writing your paragraph that you are concentrating on showing that you understand the writers' methods of presentation, the effects created and the writers' purposes.

1 Compare the ways the writers use non-standard English in *'from* Unrelated Incidents' and 'Half-Caste'.

2 Compare the methods the writers use to present the ways the speakers feel in 'Not My Business' and 'Presents from my Aunts in Pakistan'.

3 Compare the effects created by the layout of the poems in *'from* Search For My Tongue' and *'from* Unrelated Incidents'.

Use of textual detail and comparison

Another typical question on Cluster 2 might be:

Compare the effects created by breaking the rules of conventional standard English in 'from *Unrelated Incidents' and 'Half-Caste'.*

Activity 17

Looking at the two poems *'from* Unrelated Incidents' and 'Half-Caste', either discuss or jot down answers to the following questions.

1 Why do you think Tom Leonard chose to set out his poem in the way that he did?

2 Look at the punctuation and the lack of upper-case letters. Why do you think he made these choices?

3 How does the Scottish dialect fit in with what he is saying in the poem as a whole?

4 What do you think Leonard's feelings are at different points in the poem?

5 What words and phrases suggest what you think?

6 Most of the poem 'Half-Castle' is in Caribbean dialect. Identify the parts that are in standard English.

7 Why has Agard made these choices?

8 Identify the different kinds of repetition. What is the effect of each of them?

9 Look at what punctuation there is and the lack of it most of the time. Why do you think Agard made these choices?

Finally,

10 Using your answers from questions 1–9, write one paragraph on the following topic. Concentrate on making comparisons and supporting these with textual detail.

Compare the effects created by breaking the rules of conventional standard English in 'from *Unrelated Incidents' and 'Half-Caste'.*

Activity 18

1 Now use the mark scheme descriptors to see the level of skills you are achieving in your answer to question 10 in Activity 17.

Notional D
- range of comment supported by textual details with some valid cross-reference.

Notional C
- range of extended supported comment with some developed cross-reference.

Notional B
- effective use of textual detail with integrated cross-reference.

2 Rewrite your answer if you did not achieve a C or a B.

Activity 19

Have a go at writing one paragraph on each of the following questions.

Remember when you are writing your paragraph that you are concentrating on using textual details effectively and making a range of developed comparisons.

1 Compare the effects created by the choices of structure made by Leonard and Osundare in 'from Unrelated Incidents' and 'Not My Business'.

2 Compare the methods used to present people in 'Presents from my Aunts in Pakistan' and 'Not My Business'.

3 Compare the ways the poets use the first person, 'I', in 'from Search For My Tongue' and 'Half-Caste'.

The Assessment Objective as a whole

Now that you have looked at each of the skills in turn it is time to put them all together.

Let's find out what you already know about 'Presents from my Aunts in Pakistan' and 'from Search For My Tongue'.

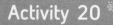

Activity 20

1 Either jot down or discuss answers to the following questions.

 a What do you think each poem is about?

 b What do you learn about the point of view of the speaker during the course of the poem?

 c What methods do the poets use to present these ideas and points of view?

2 Now discuss or jot down:

 a what you think the cultural differences are in these poems

 b what the poets have to say about identity

 c the methods they use to do these things.

3 Now write your answer in full to the following question:

 Compare the methods the poets use to present identity in 'from Search For My Tongue' and 'Presents from my Aunts in Pakistan'.

Examiner hints

• You don't have to have lots of comparisons. About three will be enough and then you can fill them out and develop them as you are writing your essay.

• Make sure that you remember the three different things the examiners are looking for:

 – response to feelings, attitudes and ideas

 – the poets' methods of presentation and their effect on the reader

 – detailed textual reference and comparison.

• Aim to write about five paragraphs.

Now remind yourself of the descriptors that the examiners will be using.

Notional D	**Notional C**	**Notional B**
• awareness of feeling(s), attitude(s), idea(s) • range of comments supported by textual details with some valid cross-reference • comment on effects achieved by writers.	• understanding of feelings, attitudes, ideas • range of extended supported comment with some developed cross-reference • awareness of writers' techniques and purposes.	• appreciation of feelings, attitudes, ideas • effective use of textual detail with integrated cross-reference • understanding of a variety of writers' techniques and purposes.

Read the extract on the next page, taken from a student's answer. Look at the examiner's annotations to see how the mark scheme descriptors have been applied.

I think 'Presents from my Aunts in Pakistan' says a lot about identity because she receives elaborate Pakistani clothing from her aunts but she does not really like the clothes because she feels 'alien in the sitting room' and is ashamed to wear the clothes in front of her school friend. She also talks about how the Pakistani jewellery 'drew blood', showing how she felt about her previous culture.

— Extended supported comment

There is also dramatic language in 'from Search For My Tongue' where Sujata Bhatt uses the metaphor of a plant to describe her original language which she fears 'rots and dies'. The word 'rot' is repeated twice to provoke an emotional reaction and to shock the reader into imagining what losing your language feels like.

— Method
— Method
— Method
— Effect

Both poets are confused about their identities. Sujata Bhatt is frightened about losing her original language, although she does remember it, and Moniza Alvi finds it hard to decide whether to identify with her country of origin or with where she is living now.

— Valid cross-reference
— Supported

What did the examiner think?

The student's answer above is notionally a Grade D answer.

To get a notional C the student needs to:

- be more precise in the comparisons
- write more about the effects of the writers' choices
- be more accurate and precise about the similarities and differences between the poets' methods of presenting identity
- comment on the writers' purposes.

To get a notional B the student needs to:
- examine a range of comparisons, based on the poets' methods
- show appreciation of a range of the writers' techniques of presentation
- develop an argument through the essay
- make sure that the examples, details and comparisons are integrated with the argument
- show understanding of the writers' purposes.

Activity 21

If you haven't already achieved a C or a B, rewrite your own answer to question 3 of Activity 20.

What have I learnt?

Check that you:
- know how to answer the poetry questions
- know what the examiners are looking for.

In the future you:
- can practise these skills either individually or together on any pair of poems
- could do this once a day or even once every two days between now and the exam; you would know the poems really well and be very well prepared for the exam.

Writing

10 Sentence structures

Getting started

The simplest definition of a sentence is that it has to contain a subject and a main verb ('doing' or 'state of mind' word).

There are three different kinds of sentence: simple, compound and complex.

- A **simple** sentence has a subject and a main verb, e.g. *I went shopping.*
- A **compound** sentence is a series of simple sentences joined together (usually with 'and' or 'but'), e.g. *I went shopping and bought Bill a birthday present.*
- A **complex** sentence is longer with one part dependent on another (using what is called a subordinating conjunction like 'although', 'because', 'until'), e.g. *I went shopping because I needed to buy Bill a birthday present.*

Activity 1

Decide which kind of sentence each of the following is.

1 I am happy.

2 I went into town.

3 Although I went into town, I spent most of the day at home.

4 I went into town and did the shopping.

5 A visit to the bank was necessary because I had almost run out of money.

6 I did the shopping and met my friends.

7 I did the shopping and met my friends before we all went out to the cinema.

In addition to these sentences, writers sometimes use a sentence that doesn't have a verb in it. This is called a **minor** sentence and is usually used for some kind of dramatic effect to jolt the reader. For example:

> When I got home I realised that he had not only taken my bank card and shopping list, but that he had also taken my door keys. Gutted!

'*Gutted*!' is the minor sentence here. Don't use minor sentences too often and make sure they are for a particular effect.

Advice from the examiner

1 Writing that interests the reader will have a variety of sentence structures, and this is what the examiner is looking for in the exam. The examiner is also looking for you using 'sentence forms for effect'. This means that you are choosing a particular kind of sentence structure because you know it will have an impact on the reader. It often takes the form of a very short sentence following on from several longer sentences.

2 You will also notice that every sentence ends in a full stop – or in an alternative such as a question mark or exclamation mark. The most common mistake in the exam is to put a comma where there should be a full stop (called a 'comma splice'). These mistakes are usually made not because the student doesn't know any better, but because they are thinking about saying the next thing rather than concentrating on how the sentence is written.

3 Try to get used to thinking in terms of sentence units when you are writing. This will force you to use a full stop when the sentence ends. If you have made a plan, then you know what you are going to write next. So then you can concentrate on putting your full stops in the right places and you won't make so many mistakes with comma splices.

Activity 2

Read the following paragraph from a student explaining the importance of a childhood memory.

> This memory was very important to me. It made me feel that I was growing up. It taught me that my parents were really important. It made me much more able to rely on myself. It made me able to make decisions for myself.

These are perfectly decent sentences, but:

- they are all simple sentences
- they are all the same length
- there are no links between them
- they do little to interest the reader.

Rewrite the student's paragraph, so that you interest readers by giving them a range of sentence structures. You can rearrange and re-sequence the sentences if you want to.

Activity 3

1   Imagine you are daydreaming in a classroom with a window. Describe what you can see outside the window. Concentrate on creating a variety of sentence structures. Write for 10 minutes.

2   When you have finished, identify the kinds of sentences you or a partner have used. Highlight and annotate examples of:

- a simple sentence
- a compound sentence
- a complex sentence
- a minor sentence
- using sentence forms for effect (see 'Advice from the examiner' on pages 92–93).

3   Rewrite what you have done if your piece does not contain all of the above different types of sentence.

Examiner hints

- You should not write to a formula every time, where you are making sure you have everything in your answer.
- However, you do need variety of sentence structure in your exam answer.
- You also need to use some sentence forms for effect.
- This means that you are thinking about the reader, not just about the content that you are putting down on the page.

Now read examples A–D from students attempting this same task.

Student A

Outside I can see a large tree with lots of leaves. It hasn't lost its leaves yet. In the distance are some sheep. They make the landscape look dotted with white. If you went up to them they wouldn't be white, though. They would be grey with dirt at this time of year. I can also see some goalposts. No one is playing football yet. It's still the morning. Everyone is inside. I wish I wasn't.

Student B

> Outside, the tree still has lots of leaves because it hasn't lost them yet. In the distance the sheep make the landscape look dotted with white, even though they are really grey with the muck of summer. The goalposts on the playing field are deserted. It's morning so no one is kicking the ball around yet because they are all inside in lessons. I wish I wasn't.

Student C

> Outside I can see a large tree with lots of leaves and in the distance are some sheep. They make the landscape look dotted with white, but if you went up to them they wouldn't be white. They would be grey at this time of year. I can also see some goalposts but no one is playing football yet. It's still the morning and everyone is inside. I wish I wasn't.

Student D

> Outside, the tree. It's still got all its leaves because they haven't fallen yet. I wish I was outside, further than the tree. Sheep in the distance are dotting the landscape with white even though they are grey with the summer's grime. They are chasing each other, playing, unlike the kids in school, trapped inside, leaving the goalposts on the playing field deserted. Wish I was outside.

Here are the mark scheme descriptors that the examiners will be using to mark your answers:

D/E	B/C
• uses a range of securely demarcated sentence structures.	• uses a range of securely demarcated sentence structures • uses sentence forms for effect.

In order to fulfil the D/E band descriptors you have to:
- use a range of sentence structures
- use punctuation accurately especially at the ends of the sentences.

In order to fulfil the B/C descriptors you have to:
- use a range of sentence structures
- punctuate them correctly
- use sentence forms for effect.

Activity 4

1   You now have five examples to analyse – your own and the four student responses on pages 94–95. Look closely at the five examples to see which mark scheme descriptors they meet. Remember that you are concentrating on looking at the use of sentence structures and of sentence forms for effect.

2   If you have not met the targets for the B/C band, rewrite what you have written, bearing in mind what you need to demonstrate.

What have I learnt?

Check that you:
- know how to use a variety of sentence structures in your writing
- know how to use sentence forms for effect
- know that you need to think in sentence units in order to get the punctuation right at the end of the sentences
- know what the examiners are looking for
- can use the mark scheme descriptors to make sure that your work falls into the higher band.

In the future you:
- can practise writing 10-minute pieces thinking about sentence structure
- can gradually increase this time.

11 Spelling

My learning

This chapter will help you to:

- spell as accurately as you can
- identify errors you often make
- check and revise your work
- improve your responses in the exam.

Assessment Objective

- Use accurate spelling.

A lot of students think it's the teacher's job to find the spelling mistakes in their work. It isn't. It's your job, because in the exam the teacher isn't there to do it for you! Only if you get lots of practice in finding your own mistakes will you be able to do this in the exam.

Advice from the examiner

More than half the spelling mistakes in the exam are what examiners would call 'carelessness'. Often the same word is spelt different ways when it is used more than once. Often the word is correctly spelt in the other half of the paper. You must get used to finding the words that you know how to spell, and correcting them. Your task in the exam hasn't finished when you've got to the end of the writing. Checking and correcting are vital if you are going to do yourself justice.

Examiner hint

Spelling is very individual. There is no quick and easy way to improve your spelling; it takes hard work. The best thing to do is to keep a spelling notebook if you have trouble with your spelling.

You should:

- write down the words you misspell
- look up the correct spellings in a dictionary
- learn the spellings of words you frequently misspell.

Activity 1

Read the following extract from a task written by a student in exam conditions. The student didn't check or correct their work at all. Then complete the following task.

Make a list of the words that are misspelt and see how many of them you can correct. Use a dictionary to check any that you are uncertain about, and note down the correct spelling.

Dear Editor

Your newspaper has been carrying a lot of articals recently which make criticisums of young people. This is unfair and upsetting to those of us who live perfectly law-abiding lives.

You have critisised us for loitering in public places, for terrorising old people, for dawbing public buildings with grafiti and for stealing from corner shops. Admitedly a small minority of teenegers do this; we in the majority don't. We are apalled by anti-social behaviour and want to make our town a better and safer place to live in. To receive criticisum all the time is bad for our moral and tars us all with the same brush. Your newspaper has run several articles about the dangers of sterotiping but here is a prime example of it.

Please write some articles drawing attension to the acheivements of young people. Write about are hard work at school, are work for charity and are good cittizenship.

Yours faithfuly,
A student

Examiner hint

Add to your notebook those words in the student's letter that you weren't able to spell correctly.

Because this student's letter is otherwise well written, it is a great shame that the spelling lets this student down.

Activity 2

Read the following, which is a recent exam question:

Choose something you are interested in and know a lot about and write in such a way as to inform the examiner about it.

In response to this question, choose a topic and write for about 10 minutes on that topic in order to inform the reader about it.

Use as wide a range of interesting words as you can.

Examiner hint

Even though you are going to be looking at your spelling, don't limit your choices to simple words or words you know how to spell. Pick the best and the most interesting words you can, because another part of the assessment is about the range of vocabulary that you choose.

Activity 3

Here are the mark scheme descriptors that examiners will be using to mark your answer.

D/E	**B/C**
• some accurate spelling of more complex words.	• generally secure in spelling.

1 Re-read your answer to Activity 2 and use these mark scheme descriptors to see which band you are in for spelling.

2 Go through your work carefully to see how many words you have misspelt and can correct. You may need to swap your answer with another student. Remember that in the exam about three-quarters of misspelt words are words the students know very well how to spell.

3 Look up in a dictionary the spelling of any words whose spelling you are not sure of.

Examiner hint

From your work in Activities 2 and 3, add any words whose spelling you were not sure of to your spelling notebook.

What have I learnt?

Check that you:

- know how to find spelling mistakes in the work of others
- can find your own spelling mistakes
- know what the examiners are looking for
- can use the mark scheme descriptors to make sure that your work is in the higher band.

In the future you:

- can find your own mistakes
- can keep an ongoing spelling notebook
- can continue to improve your spelling.

12 Punctuation

My learning

This chapter will help you to:

- use a range of punctuation
- use punctuation accurately
- check and revise your work
- improve your responses in the exam.

Assessment Objective:

- Use accurate punctuation.

Getting started

To help you use accurate punctuation you should know that:

- a full stop (or question mark or exclamation mark) comes at the end of every sentence: .
- what people say, and book titles, are in inverted commas: ' ' (or " ")
- commas separate items in a list or denote a pause in a sentence (usually where there is a subordinating clause), or act in pairs instead of brackets: ,
- question marks come at the end of every question: **?**
- exclamation marks come after an exclamation: **!**
- a colon introduces a list: :
- a semi-colon separates full sentences that are closely interrelated and interdependent in meaning: **;**
- apostrophes show missing letters or possesssion: **'**

Commas, full stops and capital letters

It's rare to find students who don't know where to put full stops, commas and capital letters. Most mistakes that are made in the exam are when they are concentrating on what they are saying rather than how they are saying it. The trick, then, is to work out what you are going to say in a sentence before you begin to write it, so that when you are writing you can concentrate on putting it as effectively and as accurately as you can.

Read the passage on page 102 to see how it illustrates the rules that appear around the text.

Each new sentence starts with a capital letter

Capital letters are used for the main words in titles

Commas separate items in a list except for the last two which are joined by 'and'

Commas in pairs separate off from the rest of the sentence something that could have been put in brackets

Capital letters are also used for names

Each sentence ends with a full stop (or question mark or exclamation mark).

A comma is used after 'however' if it starts a sentence

A comma sometimes denotes a pause in the sentence, usually before a new clause is introduced

> Accurate punctuation helps the reader to follow what is being said. Lynn Truss made this clear in her book 'Eats Shoots and Leaves'. She showed how inaccurate punctuation confuses the reader, creates ambiguities and is a sign of sloppy thinking. However, clear and accurate punctuation makes reading easy. Pairs of commas, showing that items placed between them are separate from the rest of the sentence, help the reader to keep the main point in mind. Although Lynn Truss's book is actually a serious book about accuracy in writing, she makes it amusing to read.

Activity 1

Identify which of the above rules is exemplified by each of the following examples, all taken from a newspaper article entitled 'Need an Autumn Break?'. The first one is done for you.

1 Travel, as any philosopher or fool will tell you, is what you make of it.
   Rules 1, 4 and 7.

2 You could be sitting in an aluminium box, eight miles above the Arctic Circle, squabbling with your partner.

3 You could be herded through the Alhambra, the Louvre or Machu Picchu so quickly and in such a vast crowd that you feel you've scarcely seen it.

4 Or you can stop, think about what it means to travel and just start looking outside your front door.

5 Here's a little test for you.

6 Can you name the nearest Area of Outstanding Natural Beauty to your house?

7 What about the nearest forest?

8 Or the nearest house?

9 The nearest canal?

10 There you go.

11 That's the next few weekends sorted.

Activity 2

The full stops, commas and capital letters have been omitted from the opening of the following newspaper article.

Write out the passage correctly, putting the full stops, commas and capital letters in the right places.

for the first time we have an all english champion's league final recently england has attracted some of the most talented players in the world attracted by the money the challenge and the publicity these players have made the premier league the best in europe for liverpool and manchester united fans none of this matters for them the trip to moscow is simply an unforgettable experience

Apostrophes

Apostrophes are used in two cases:
1 To show that a letter is missing, e.g. can't (short for cannot).
2 To show possession, e.g. Janet's (meaning 'belonging to Janet').

Missing letters

Activity 3

1 Find and copy out the examples of apostrophes to show missing letters in the following passage.

I can't help but think that I'm going to improve my punctuation skills by concentrating hard on it. In fact we're all going to improve. That's because we're going to be thinking about detail and because we know that we can't afford to make too many mistakes. It's not hard, really.

2 Now write out the words that would be there if the apostrophe was not being used. For example: *I'm = I am.*

Possession

The rules here are quite straightforward. If it belongs to something singular, then write the word, add the apostrophe and add an 's'. For example:

- *the pig's trotters* – the trotters belonging to one pig
- *your heart's desire* – the desire belonging to your heart
- *the class's classroom* – the classroom belonging to one class.

If it belongs to something plural ending in 's', then write the word and add an apostrophe. For example:

- *the pigs' trotters* – the trotters belonging to more than one pig
- *their hearts' desires* – their desires belonging to their hearts
- *the classes' classroom* – the classroom belonging to more than one class.

If, however, it belongs to something plural that doesn't end in an 's', then write the word, add an apostrophe and add an 's'. For example:

- *the children's books*
- *the sheep's pasture.*

The only exception to these rules covers a class of words called possessives. These words carry the idea of possession inside them and so they don't have an apostrophe. Here they are:

- *yours, his, hers, its, theirs, ours.*

If you follow these simple rules then you can't go wrong with apostrophes. Remember, however:

- *its* means 'belonging to it'
- *it's* means 'it is'.

Activity 4

Just to check that you have got the idea, put the apostrophes in the right places if and when they are needed in the following examples.

1   Its not enough just to write your answer.
2   Youve got to make sure that you check carefully.
3   Students errors often lead to their underperformance.
4   Almost every piece of work in the exam has its errors.
5   The examiners report often mentions such errors.

Question marks and exclamation marks

Remember:

- a question mark is needed at the end of every direct question
- an exclamation is a shout, so use an exclamation mark when something is shouted or when something is a shock or surprise.

Direct questions are those that are asking a question.
For example: 'Where are you going?' or 'Why are exams necessary?'.

Some students tend to over-use exclamation marks. One is plenty. Don't decorate the page by doubling or trebling them. If you think about the 'shout', then you will be safe. For example 'Then I fell asleep' doesn't need an exclamation mark but 'Ouch!' does.

Colons and semi-colons

The **colon** is used:

- to introduce a list
- to introduce quoted direct speech.

You should be very confident about using colons if you have read much of this book. There are hundreds of them because I've used lots of lists. Most of these lists, though, are in bullet point form. I could have put them in continuous prose instead, in which case the colon would have introduced the list and then the items would have been separated from one another by commas except for the last two which would have been linked by 'and'.

For example the 'Check your answer' list after Activity 2 on page 103 could have been written like this:

Either on your own, or swapping with a partner, make sure that you have: a capital letter for the beginning of each sentence, a capital letter for the three names, commas separating the items in lists (except for the last two, which are joined by 'and' instead) and commas in pairs where they are used instead of brackets.

The **semi-colon** is used in two cases:

- where two full sentences are very closely linked
- where a colon has introduced a list and the items in the list are grammatically full sentences. When this is the case these items in the list are separated by semi-colons rather than commas.

Activity 5

Here are two sentences that need colons and semi-colons. Each example is numbered. Decide whether a colon or a semi-colon should go in each place.

1   There were many sides to William Shakespeare (1) actor, playwright, husband, father and property owner.

2   There were many sides to William Shakespeare (1) he was an actor (2) he wrote plays (3) he was a husband and father and he was a property owner.

Inverted commas

These are used in two situations:
- around direct speech
- around the title of a film, short story, play, poem or book (except for the Bible and the Qur'an).

All direct speech (a quotation of what exactly someone said) has to have inverted commas round it. But when you are writing dialogue, remember that each new speaker must be in a new paragraph.

The following extract from Doris Lessing's 'Flight' shows speech set out correctly:

He stumped his feet alternately, thump, thump, on the wooden floor and shouted: "She'll marry him. I'm telling you, she'll be marrying him next!"

His daughter rose swiftly, brought him a cup, set him a plate.

"Now, now," she crooned. "What's wrong with him? Why not?"

"She's eighteen. Eighteen!"

"I was married at seventeen and I never regretted it."

Bringing it all together

Activity 6

1 Write for 10 minutes on the following task, making sure that you use a range of punctuation correctly:

   Persuade your class that they should go on a trip to a theme park.

2 Carefully check your work to make sure that you get rid of any errors you have made.

3 Now check your work against the mark scheme descriptors.

D/E
- starts to use a range of punctuation.

B/C
- uses a range of punctuation
- generally secure in punctuation which clarifies meaning and purpose.

Which band do you think your answer is in?

Examiner hints

In order to be in the D/E band for punctuation you have to be able to:

- use a range of punctuation.

That means using at least three different punctuation marks correctly.

In order to be in the B/C band you have to be:

- generally secure in punctuation which clarifies meaning and purpose.

The wider the range of punctuation, and the more accurate it is, the better.

What have I learnt?

Check that you:
- know how to use a range of punctuation
- can use a range of punctuation accurately
- know what the examiners are looking for
- can use the mark band descriptors to make sure your work is in the higher band.

In the future you:
- can pay close attention to how punctuation is used in any texts that you read
- can practise checking your own punctuation in everything that you write.

13 Use and adapt forms

My learning

This chapter will help you to:

- think about the form required for your response
- remind yourself of key features of some of the main forms
- improve your response in the exam.

Assessment Objective

- Use and adapt forms for different readers and purposes.

Getting started

We don't write everything in the same way. How we write depends very much on purpose and audience. Each time you write you make choices about:

- form (see below for different sorts of forms)
- presentation
- language
- sentence structures
- presentational features such as paragraphs, bullet points, headlines.

In GCSE English you look at a wide range of forms of media and non-fiction writing. Many of these will have been in preparation for the unseen Reading section of Paper 1, but their features are also useful to you when you are producing your own writing, both for coursework and in the exam on both papers.

Some main forms that you are likely to be asked about in the exam include:

- reports
- articles
- letters
- information sheets
- advice sheets
- diary entries.

You may be asked to write in any of these forms in the exam.

Activity 1

There are many different ways of presenting information. Represent the information in the box in these three different ways:

1 in a paragraph
2 as bullet pointed information
3 with headings and sub-headings.

> The Manchester United striker, Wayne Rooney, is looking on the bright side of England failing to qualify for Euro 2008.
>
> He can have a summer wedding.
>
> He can also now have a honeymoon.
>
> If England had qualified the wedding would have to have been later.
>
> Coleen McLoughlin, a model, has been looking at venues with her mum and a wedding organiser.
>
> Wayne is reported as saying that Coleen, 21, is in charge.
>
> They have been round England, France and Italy.
>
> They plan to look in Ireland and another place in England.
>
> Wayne and Coleen plan to marry in June 2008.

Examiners will be more interested in the text you write than in the layout, so don't waste time with elaborate pictures and page design. But you might want to use some key features, such as a headline for an article, sub-headings if they are useful, the correct way to set out a letter and so on. But don't put your writing in columns if you are writing an article.

Letters

Remind yourself of some of the key features of a letter:
• what addresses you put in
• where the addresses go
• how you start the letter
• how you sign off the letter.

All these will depend on the purpose and the audience.

On the next page is an example of the beginning of a formal letter written to a company.

10 River Street —— Your address top right
Hasleton
Manchester
M26 3AY

30 April 2008 —— The date, beneath your address

Customer Services Manager —————— The address of the company/
Spendmoney   person you are writing to
42 The Highway   lower down and on the left
Birmingham
B2 8AW

Dear Sir/Madam ———————————— In this instance, as the name
                                   isn't known, Dear Sir/Madam
                                   is used – so this letter would
                                   end 'Yours faithfully'

A letter to someone at a company whose name you know might start 'Dear Mr Jones'. In this case the letter would end 'Yours sincerely'.

A letter to a friend would start more informally, possibly with 'Hi'. It would also end more informally, possibly with 'Love' or 'Cheers'.

Activity 2

Write the beginning (address or addresses and greeting) and ending of a letter for each of the following:

a   a formal letter accompanying a job application

b   a letter to a friend

c   a letter replying to one from Mrs A Patel at the Customer Services department of a supermarket

d   a business letter to someone whose name you do not know.

Check your answer

Have you used the following correctly:

- Dear Sir/Madam, Dear Mrs Patel, Hi mate
- Yours sincerely, Yours faithfully, Love
- your own address and the address of the person and place the letter is going to for a formal letter
- just your address for an informal letter?

Other forms

You will vary your language according to the purpose and audience of your writing. Read each of the texts below, then complete Activity 3 on the next page.

A

X Factor vote row

OFCOM will investigate complaints about *The X Factor* final after viewers said that they could not get through to vote for Rhydian Roberts, who was runner-up (Adam Sherwin writes). The Welsh singer had been the favourite to win but lost to Leon Jackson on Saturday night's ITV1 show, watched by 12 million people. Ofcom has received 80 complaints so far.

The programme denied any irregularities. Talkback Thames, the producers, said some viewers had experienced an engaged tone but blamed it on the high number of calls. ITV admitted overcharging *X Factor* viewers by £200,000 last year, when 1.3 million votes were mistakenly charged at the wrong rate.

B

Hi m8 hows u? U wanna meet @ 6 tonite? Got freebys 4 gig @ Nitehouse.

C

The Present Song

There are no presents under the Christmas tree.
Who'll put a present underneath the tree?
I'll put a present underneath the tree.
What is your present underneath the tree?

Gold and myrrh and frankincense.
Dates and nuts and chocolate.
Socks and ties and aftershave.
Dogs and cats and guinea pigs.
One tangerine.
Soap and scent and bubblebath.
Books and toys and DVDs.
Port and wine and armagnac.
Hats and gloves and cardigans.
Drums and flutes and pipes and harps and
Jingle bells, jingle bells.
Rings and jewels and necklaces.
Gold and myrrh and frankincense.

D

COMMUNITY MUSICIAN FOR CLASE AND CAEMAWR?

Another of the Morriston Phoenix Choir's exciting plans is to get a 'Community Musician' in place in the Clase/Caemawr area by January 2008.

The idea is that the appointed person will run sessions to encourage and train singing and instrumental groups of all ages in the area.

It is hoped that they might also get other ventures off the ground next year, such as a musically biased pantomime with local people participating.

More news on this, soon, we hope.

E

YOU CAN'T BEA THAT DAFT

PRINCESS   Beatrice stunned passengers on a Eurostar train when she declared: 'I thought Dover was in Cornwall.'

She made the remark about the Kent town as she returned from a boozy trip to Brussels with pals. One of the group said: 'We must be near Dover.'

Bea, 19, replied: 'Dover? I thought Dover was in Cornwall or Devon.' A passenger said: 'Everyone fell about. We weren't sure if she was having a laugh.'

Meanwhile her mum Fergie has admitted she felt she let the Queen down.

She told *Hello!* Magazine: 'I got fat, I had debts, I got totally out of control with myself.'

Miles out … Beatrice

Activity 3

1   When you have read texts A–E, match them to one of each of the following types of writing:
   - a tabloid newspaper
   - a broadsheet newspaper
   - a poem
   - a text message
   - a community newsletter.

2   Now make a list of features that are typical of each of the five forms you have just identified. Make sure you make some detail about each of the following:
   - layout
   - sentence structure
   - vocabulary
   - paragraphing
   - punctuation
   - variety of presentation.

Sometimes in the exam you will be told what sort of article to write and who the audience is. Sometimes, though, the choice is yours, so you have to think about the choices that you would make.

Activity 4

1 Imagine that you have been asked to write an article. Make a list of the choices such as language use or punctuation, that you would make for publication in each of the following:
   - a tabloid newspaper
   - a broadsheet newspaper
   - a local newspaper
   - a special interest magazine.

2 Now choose a topic that interests you and write about 12 to 15 lines for each of the four types of publication listed in question 1. Concentrate on the different choices you would make for each of the following:
   - layout
   - vocabulary
   - sentence structure
   - sentence length
   - paragraphing
   - punctuation.

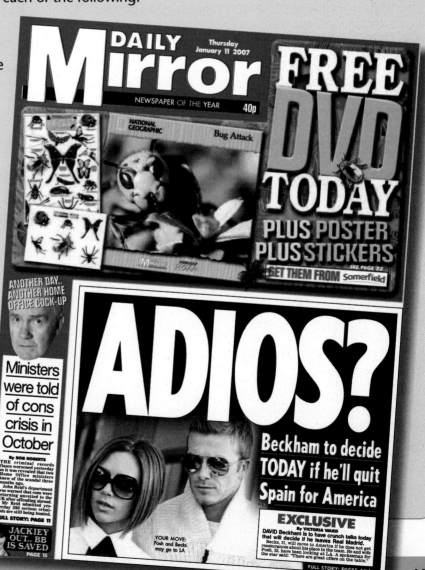

Activity 5

Imagine that one of your close friends has moved away and that you have been invited to a party where they are now living. Lots of other people are interested in what has happened to this person and so you have decided that you want to write to tell them about their friend and to describe the party.

Here is a list of the people you are going to write to:

- your gran
- your friend's previous teacher
- your friend's ex girl- or boyfriend
- your uncle in Australia.

These are your options:

- a letter
- a note
- an email.

For each of the four people, write for about 10 minutes, thinking carefully about:

- what you choose to tell them
- the language you use
- the kinds of sentences you use
- the conventions of written English you choose.

Examiner hints

It is unlikely that you will be asked to write a text message or an email in the exam. But it is important that you know how these kinds of informal writing differ from the more formal kinds of writing that you will be asked to do in the exam.

Activity 6

Now imagine that you have been away on a week's holiday. You kept a diary because you wanted to remember what happened (although you might not want other people to see everything you wrote).

You also want to enter a competition run by the local newspaper for reports of holidays.

Write for 10 minutes to show the choices you would make for each of these:

1 the diary entry

2 the report for the local newspaper.

Think carefully about:

- what you reveal
- the tone and register
- the way the writing is organised
- the language you choose
- the sentence length and sentence structures you use.

What have I learnt?

Check that you can make choices every time you write about:

- purpose
- audience
- language
- sentence structure
- tone
- the form of the writing.

In the future:

- practise these skills whatever piece you are writing (it doesn't have to be for English).

14 Organise ideas

My learning

This chapter will help you to:

- check that you are writing in sentences
- place paragraphs effectively
- write whole texts
- improve your response in the exam.

Assessment Objective

- Organise ideas into sentences, paragraphs and whole texts.

The four key stages that you need to go through in order to produce a successful piece of writing are:

- thinking • planning • writing • checking and improving.

Organise ideas into sentences

Chapter 10 looked at using a range of sentence structures effectively, focusing particularly on:

- simple sentences
- compound sentences
- complex sentences
- minor sentences
- using a range of sentence structures.

You need to understand how to use all of these in order to help organise your ideas into sentences. Look again at this chapter if you are not yet confident with these sentence structures.

Organise ideas into paragraphs

You also need to know that effective paragraphing:

- divides the writing into sections to make for easy reading
- introduces new aspects of the topic in new paragraphs
- has links between the paragraphs.

The article on page 117 has been annotated, with comments about the paragraphs. Read the article, together with the annotations, and look closely at where a new paragraph begins and why.

Opening section introducing Sister Wendy

Sister Wendy Beckett is feeling 'a bit wobbly' when we meet in the marbled reception of a smart London hotel. Life at her convent starts at 1.30am and she is usually in bed by 6pm, so her body clock today is all over the place. Taking my hand for support, the 77-year-old nun is exactly as she looks on TV, sporting the style of all-enveloping traditional garb that only the chorus line in *The Sound of Music* wear these days. She has long, strikingly white fingers, with very soft skin but a firm grip.

This paragraph concerns an incident just after the writer has met Sister Wendy

She is still holding on to me as we slowly make our way towards a quiet corner when a sun-tanned woman runs up to us at a rather alarming pace. 'I have to speak to this lady,' she announces in a Scandinavian accent, grabbing Sr Wendy's free hand. 'I'm Karen, and you have changed my life.' She looks as if she is about to cry. 'Watching your programmes has changed my life. I'm so grateful.'

New paragraph links the meeting in the previous paragraph with some background about Sister Wendy's achievements in television

What she's referring to is a series of documentaries, mostly about the fine arts, that Sr Wendy made in her sixties. Her brief appearance in a TV arts slot in 1991 caught the commissioners' eyes and prompted a run of programmes that made her, alongside Mother Teresa of Calcutta and Maria von Trapp, the most instantly recognisable nun in the world. There was even a West End musical, *Postcards from God*, based on her life.

Sister Wendy now

Perhaps the new paragraph here helps the reader to take in what Sister Wendy says. It isn't really necessary as it continues her speech from the previous paragraph

Of late, though, her public has had to make do with just the occasional talk – 'the thing that I hate doing most in the world' – and books. She has agreed to travel up to town to talk about her latest paperback, *Sister Wendy on Prayer*. 'I don't come out for pleasure. People ring and say 'Would you like to have lunch?' and it would be very nice but I have to say no.

'I come out of the convent very, very rarely. As rarely as possible, in fact. I hope that woman doesn't write to me. My time is for God. I've no time for gardening and letter-writing, the usual let-outs for those who are alone.'

Comment on what Sister Wendy said. In a short paragraph on its own for dramatic effect

It comes out in her high, kindly voice, but there is an unmistakable edge to the observation; not quite what you expect in a nun.

Background information and Sister Wendy's history

Sr Wendy has spent the past 37 years away from the world as a hermit and consecrated virgin, living in a caravan in a copse in the monastery garden of the enclosed Carmelite convent at Quidenham in Norfolk. Before that, she was a teaching nun in her native South Africa with the Notre Dame de Namur order, but had to give up after a series of epileptic seizures, brought on by stress.

Development of Sister Wendy's career

It makes her parallel life as a television icon all the more extraordinary. Initially, at Quidenham, she spent her time translating medieval Latin texts (she had been awarded a Congratulatory First by Oxford in 1953), but by the 1980s had begun writing spiritual meditations on contemporary art. Some were circulated among a small group of friends and came to the attention of Delia Smith, who, as well as her well-known enthusiasm for cooking and Norwich Football Club, is a connoisseur of fine religious writing. She persuaded newspapers to publish them, and soon after the documentary-makers came calling.

From *The Daily Telegraph*, 18 October 2007

There aren't any hard and fast rights and wrongs about paragraphing. Where you put one is a matter of choice. What is important is that you know why you made the decisions you did and that they were effective choices.

Activity 1

On the opposite page is the beginning of a newspaper article about a television series. It has been presented here with no paragraphs at all. Your task is to identify where the best places would be to have new paragraphs and to think why you have chosen these places. The first two paragraphs have been done for you below.

STANDING in a Methodist chapel, I am wearing a cloche hat, silk scarf and gloves, while around me a congregation dressed in their faded Sunday best sing hymns in Welsh.

As the minister delivers his sermon, preaching against the evils of gambling and Halloween, dirty-faced toddlers in tweed suits and cloth caps try to wriggle free from their mothers' arms. Someone passes round a collection plate to help the families of men killed or injured in mining accidents. Few can afford to give anything.

From the *Daily Mail*, 6 November 2007

Check your answer

A long text needs to be broken up into sections in order to make it easy to take in. A well-paragraphed piece makes for easy reading and helps you to take the article in sections.
It also helps you to identify the different stages of the article as you read it.

Did you:

- divide the passage up into sections to help the reader take it in
- have paragraphs of different lengths
- make sure there were some links between paragraphs?

Standing in a Methodist chapel, I am wearing a cloche hat, silk scarf and gloves, while around me a congregation dressed in their faded Sunday best sing hymns in Welsh. As the minister delivers his sermon, preaching against the evils of gambling and Halloween, dirty-faced toddlers in tweed suits and cloth caps try to wriggle free from their mothers' arms. Someone passes round a collection plate to help the families of men killed or injured in mining accidents. Few can afford to give anything. I have stepped back 80 years in time to become a participant in a time-travelling experiment. In a small town called Blaenavon, high up in the Welsh Valleys, it is once again 1927. Blaenavon is the setting for *Coal House*, a new BBC reality TV show, which follows three families as they spend a month living the lives of their ancestors in the South Wales coalfield. As reality TV shows go, *Coal House* is a world away from *Big Brother* and its ilk. There are no gimmicks, no celebrity-wannabes, and there certainly isn't any lounging around. It is 1927, the year after the General Strike – a nine-day strike over wages and working conditions – which had a catastrophic impact on the coal-mining communities of Britain. The *Coal House* families are learning what it is like to live a hand-to-mouth existence, without heating, electricity or running water. It's up to the men and older boys to earn enough money to feed their families by digging for coal in the last real working mine of its kind in the UK – and that's after a four-mile walk to the pit each day. Their wages depend on how much coal they can produce by hacking away at the coal face on their hands and knees, in a cramped, pitch-black space less than one metre high. Only modern health and safety laws – for example, the 14-year-old boys aren't allowed to work underground, as they would have in 1927, and proper helmets must be worn – detract from the authenticity of the experience. The women are expected to cook meals, using the most basic ingredients (they're provided with a vegetable patch, pigs and chickens), over stoves which they must work out how to light themselves, and which provide the only source of household heat. Water has to be fetched from a pump in the square outside. They must look after their two-up, two-down mining cottages without the luxury of modern conveniences. Even the toilets are outside. And believe me, it's cold and windy in the Welsh Valleys in November. Chamber pots are provided for night-time use. Why would anybody want to put their family through this experience?

From the *Daily Mail*, 6 November 2007

Organising ideas into whole texts

Now you need to think about writing a whole text.

Activity 2

Imagine that you have been asked to write an article for a weekend colour supplement magazine about living a healthy lifestyle. Planning your response is vital. This activity takes you through the planning process before you start your full response.

1   Decide on your audience. It will be mainly adults because the magazine comes with a Sunday newspaper. It will be a general readership.

2   Brainstorm what different aspects of the topic you can cover. Do this in the form of either a list or spidergram. Here is an example of each:

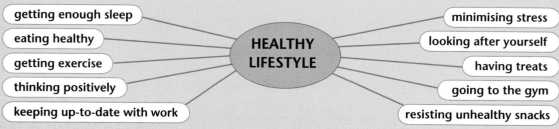

getting enough sleep

eating healthy

getting exercise

thinking positively

keeping up-to-date with work

HEALTHY LIFESTYLE

minimising stress

looking after yourself

having treats

going to the gym

resisting unhealthy snacks

When you come to write your own article, you can use some of these ideas if you wish, but feel free to add your own.

3   Decide what order to present your ideas in by numbering the different aspects of the topic. If you sequence your points well, you will be able to make some links between paragraphs. Some paragraphs will:

• develop what you've just written

• deal with a different aspect of the topic

• contrast with what you've just written.

4   Decide on your headline. Make sure it's suitable for the magazine you are writing for. You might need to leave some space and write in the headline at the end when you have finished your writing.

5   Does this sort of article need any sub-headings? It may not, but it's an issue to think about before you start.

6   Decide on:

• your opening sentence

• your last sentence.

Make sure that you make the reader want to read on by an interesting first sentence and make sure that you can think of a catchy way to end the article. You can, of course, revise both your first and your last sentence when you are checking your work, but you need to make sure they are both interesting and snappy.

Activity 3

1   Having completed Activity 2, you are now ready to write your response in full.

Aim to write for about 20 minutes, using the material you have chosen and thinking carefully about how you are writing it. While you are writing, think particularly about:

  - using a variety of sentence structures
  - starting new paragraphs in the best places
  - making links between paragraphs.

2   Now compare your response with that of a friend. Use the mark scheme descriptors below, which the examiners will be using, to help you decide how successful you and your partner have been.

Notional D	Notional C	Notional B
• clear paragraphs in sensible places.	• evidence of structure in the response as a whole • paragraphs which work well.	• well structured whole response • paragraphs which help the reader to take in the meaning • some effective links between paragraphs.

What have I learnt?

Check that you:

  - know how to use a range of sentence structures effectively
  - can put full stops at the end of each sentence
  - can use paragraphs effectively
  - can write whole texts, dividing them into paragraphs
  - can think carefully about the beginning and ending of your text.

In the future:

  - keep paragraphs in mind whatever you write, for whatever subject
  - develop the skills of making clear transitions and links between paragraphs
  - work on beginnings and endings of texts to make the reader interested.

15 Language and structure

Getting started

You will already have done a lot of work on language and structure, possibly from this book and certainly from the rest of your English studies.

Chapter 7 of this book looks closely at how linguistic devices achieve effects. Among other kinds of language, it looks at:
- verbs, nouns, adjectives, adverbs, pronouns
- alliteration, assonance, metaphor, simile.

Chapter 7 gets you to identify these linguistic devices and comment on their effect. Now you are being asked to use them in your own writing.

Chapter 8 of this book looks at structural features and considers their effects. Now it is time to use such things as:
- different kinds of sentences: simple, compound, complex, minor
- paragraphs, bullet points, sections
- introduction, conclusion
- discourse features such as 'first', 'secondly', 'in conclusion'.

Chapter 14 looks at paragraphing and the links between paragraphs.

What the examiners are looking for

The examiners are looking for:

- variety
- range of sentence structures and sentence forms for effect
- effective paragraphing
- varied and interesting vocabulary
- awareness of the effect your choices will have on a reader.

A recent exam paper set the following task:

Many people are interested in animals. Write an informative article on an animal or animals of your choice.

In order to complete this task you would need to think about:

- writing to inform
- what characteristics an article has
- an opening that engages the reader's interest right away
- paragraphs
- varied vocabulary
- a range of sentence structures.

Activity 1

Here's a reminder of the task mentioned above:

Many people are interested in animals. Write an informative article on an animal or animals of your choice.

1 Choose an animal and make a list of the different points you could make to answer the question above.

2 Number the points in your list and see how you could join some of them together by making links between paragraphs.

3 Write your answer out in full. Spend about 20 minutes on this.

Check your answer

Check the following and make improvements, if you can.

- Paragraphing
  - Have you put the paragraphs in the right places?
  - Does each one mark a clear stage in your essay?
  - Have you linked some of the paragraphs?
- Sentence structure
  - Have you used different kinds of sentence structures?
  - Have you used full stops in all the right places?
- Wide vocabulary
  - Have you used the most interesting words you can think of?
  - Have you shown off your vocabulary?
  - Have you avoided repeating the same word several times?

Now read student responses
A and B to this topic.

Student A

Have you ever been afraid of walking
around in your own house because
their all over the place. wherever you
would look they would be their doing nothing. i
am talking about the house hold cockroach they
are taking over the place. these six legged friends of
our's are reproducing like mad they are laying up to sixty
eggs a day right under our noses if they were human they
would get so much child benefit the parents would'ent even
need to go to work with the amount of money they would
be getting. these little critters are frightening us to death.
They are taking over the place one day they'll be driving
car's and kicking us out of our own houses and teaching
our kids maths and english. So we as humans should really
be careful about these insects so if you see one kill it
because you never no about the future what it might bring.

Student B

Sharks! Killing machines? Or ugly lovers? First impressions are very important and with the hit "Jaws" sharks were feard world wide, that pointy buck fin, that dark shadow could send a shiver down a sky divers, deep sea divers even any type of diver, any person for that matter. It could also put a smile on a face.

Sharks are not as bad as people think, yes they can kill and destroy but that's instinks, that's there survival technique and they know no-other, put yourself in there shoose.

38% of sharks are female and stay with there young for up to 6 years, the males move on and look after number one, they dont compete to see who the alpha-male is war scares tell the sharks fall. Many people have been attacked by sharks because they are mistaken for food (seals), once the shark has taken a bite it lets go of the human because it dosen't like the taste. When I interviewed a person who had been bitten, the first question I asked them was "why they thought it attacked them, they replied "I'm not sure, I was quite far out I was probably in their territory, sharks are not territorial they move around with the water that suits them, it has to be the right tempriture, the right season and it has to have food. Even if one of those was missing the shark would vakate another place. When I asked Dr Legen, a shark expert named "the sharkologist", when the best time to see sharks were he said to me "go out with a 20ft deep cage in mating season" So I did and the images I saw would "wow" anyone. Not one shark was aggresive. It was astonishing. The sharks we like puppies playing. Its hard to describe in words but its something everyone must experience.

The opinion on sharks will always refere to "Jaws" but until you see them for you're your own eyes your opinions are limited and worthless. So there we have it sharks can be killers when needed, partners when needed but they will always be fasonating and astonishing at every visit.

Activity 2

1 Working with a partner, go back over both of the student responses on pages 124–5. Correct what errors you can find (there are lots in both of these: spelling, full stops, other punctuation, grammar).

2 Now look at your own and your partner's responses to question 3 in Activity 1 (page 123). How effective is the:

- paragraphing
- range of sentence structure
- range of vocabulary?

Are the openings and endings interesting?

Although there are lots of errors in the work of Student A and Student B, there are also some strong points:
- variety of sentence structure
- sentence forms for effect
- interesting vocabulary choices
- phrases and surprises to interest the reader.

Think how much better both of these would be if they were more accurate. In particular, the use of full stops is weak and the sentences are not very well constructed.

What the examiners are looking for

Here are the mark scheme descriptors that relate to sentence structure, paragraphing and vocabulary. These are what the examiner uses to mark your exam answers.

Notional D	Notional C	Notional B
<ul><li>begins to engage the reader's response</li><li>clear, if mechanical paragraphing</li><li>more conscious use of vocabulary for effect.</li></ul>	<ul><li>begins to sustain reader's response</li><li>evidence of structure</li><li>usually coherent paragraphs</li><li>clear selection of vocabulary for effect.</li></ul>	<ul><li>well structured</li><li>starting to use paragraphs to enhance meaning</li><li>increasing sophistication in vocabulary choice and phrasing.</li></ul>

Activity 3

1 Use the mark scheme descriptors on page 126 to evaluate:
   - the responses from Student A and Student B
   - your own response to question 3 in Activity 1.
2 Now write some bullet point targets for Student A, Student B and yourself, identifying what each needs to aim for as far as language and structure are concerned.

What have I learnt?

Check that you:
- can identify and use aspects of language
- can identify and use paragraphs
- can identify and use a range of sentence structures
- can sequence your work effectively.

In the future:
- try to use the most interesting words you can to fit your purpose
- vary your sentence structure
- practise effective paragraphing.

16 Communicate clearly and imaginatively

My learning

This chapter will help you to:

- put all the different writing requirements together
- understand what the examiners are looking for
- improve your response in the exam.

Assessment Objective

- Communicate clearly and imaginatively.

Examiner hint

Remember that your examiner is most likely to be an English teacher coming home after a day at school to mark about 400 exam scripts in the evenings and at weekends in a three- to four-week period. Anything that you can do to make them interested in what you write and in how you write it will be to your advantage.

Getting started

So far we have looked at the different elements of what you are being tested on in Writing in Paper 1 and Paper 2:

- using a range of sentence structures effectively
- using accurate spelling
- using accurate punctuation
- adapting forms for your purpose and audience
- organising ideas into sentences, paragraphs, whole texts
- using a range of language and structural features.

This Assessment Objective, 'Communicate clearly and imaginatively', considers the six elements above to see whether they add up to:

- clear communication
- the use of your imagination.

Read the opening paragraphs from student responses A and B on the next page, together with the annotated comments from the examiner. Then complete Activity 1 on page 130.

The task the students were responding to was:

Argue for or against school uniform.

Which interests you more and why?

Student A

> Some people think that it is a good idea for pupils to wear school uniform. This is because they all then look the same and members of the public can tell what school they come from. This might be useful if they are in any trouble. On the other hand, other people think that school uniform is unnecessary because it makes everyone look the same and they are not the same they are individuals.

Clear statements arguing for school uniform, beginning to explain

Now against – not the task, which was for **or** against

Explains some arguments against but not asked for in task

Student B

> Green striped blazers and green and white ties. What could be more hideous? Instead of promoting social equality it brands all teenagers as stereotyped and ugly. How can schools expect their pupils to form good judgements, develop taste and individuality when the poor children are all forced to wear the same clothes which they would never in their wildest dreams choose to wear?

Unusual opening with clear image

Rhetorical question introduces argument against school uniform

Wide and interesting, varied vocabulary

Longer rhetorical question, complex argument; argument against school uniform clearly established

Activity 1

Looking back at the opening paragraphs by Student A and Student B, answer each of the following questions.

1. Which of these makes you interested in reading on? What techniques does it use to do so?
2. Which of these is not really answering the question?
3. Which uses language more effectively? What techniques has it used?
4. Which uses a variety of sentence structures more effectively? What kinds of sentences has it used?
5. Which shows some individuality and personality?
6. Which shows more clarity and imagination?
7. Which is more accurate technically?

What did the examiner think?

Student B answers the question, whereas Student A starts by arguing both for **and** against rather than for **or** against.

Student B's work is significantly better, more varied and more interesting than Student A's. But they are both accurate technically. There are no spelling or punctuation mistakes in either, although Student A doesn't use sentence forms for effect and only uses full stops and one comma. The examiner is unlikely to have read many like Student B's work before and so will be interested in what it is going to say. The examiner will probably have read dozens and dozens like Student A's.

Student A's is a D response, whereas Student B's would get a B.

Now read Student C's response (page 131) to the following task: *Write an article for a teenage magazine in which you **persuade** the readers not to smoke.*

> **Examiner hint**
>
> **Sentence forms for effect** are when you use a particular kind of sentence structure because it will have an impact on the reader that you are aware of. It often takes the form of a very short sentence following on from several longer sentences.

Student C

In many case smoking has lead to heart problems, lung throat and mouth cancer. Although there has been a decrease of smoking, among 15 year olds from 30% to around 23%. It is still a major problem for teenagers in britain to quit smoking. The easiest way is to not to start! However if you have, there is some urges from this magazine to stop smoking. A poll from around britain shows tat 1 in 3 of all smokers started smoking from early teens. This is a health hazard and can lead to severe problems later on in life. Could you really afford to put yourself through all that pain later on in life? Just for around 10 seconds of enjoyment a day.

Many teenagers only start smoking because their friends are, they are pressured into it or use it to calm themselves down. Is this worth taking 15 minutes off your life everytime you smoke 1 ciggarette? Smoking can't be good for you, if it causes all this damage to your body why do it?

Smoking can lead to stunting your growth and your finger tips to turn yellow. Is it really necessary, to be cool you have to smell bad, stop growing and have yellow finger tips. nice. The meaning of cool has changed a lot since my day. One of the main factors of smoking is that it makes not just you but everything and every one around you smell of smoke.

I don't know if you can live with yourself smoking for fun and killing yourself, but killing everyone around you, I couldn't live with myself for doing that.

Activity 2

Looking back at the response by Student C, answer the following questions.

1 Does it persuade teenagers not to smoke? What techniques does it use?
2 Are the points sequenced in the best way that they could be?
3 Has a range of sentence structures been used?
4 Are there any sentence forms for effect?
5 Are there any links between paragraphs?
6 Are the paragraphs in reasonable places?
7 Is there a wide range of interesting vocabulary?
8 Are words well chosen and varied enough to keep the reader interested?
9 How accurate is the spelling?
10 How accurate and varied is the punctuation?

Now you've looked at each of these student responses (A, B and C), you are in a position to look at the mark scheme that the examiners will be using.

Examiners have to give two separate marks for writing: one for communication and organisation, and one for sentence structure, punctuation and spelling.

Communication and organisation

Notional D	Notional C	Notional B
• conscious attempt to suit the needs of purpose and audience • begins to engage the reader's response.	• clear identification with purpose and audience • begins to sustain the reader's response.	• form, content and style are generally matched to purpose and audience.

Sentence structure, punctuation and spelling

D/E	B/C
• uses a range of securely demarcated sentence structures • some accurate spelling of more complex words • starts to use a range of punctuation.	• uses sentence forms for effect • generally secure in spelling • generally secure in punctuation which clarifies meaning and purpose.

Activity 3

Use the mark scheme descriptors on page 132 to form some bullet points telling Student C what they need to do to improve their work.

What have I learnt?

Check that you:

- know what the examiners are looking for
- can use the mark scheme descriptors to help you look for strengths and weaknesses in your own work and that of others.

In the future:

- identify the skills where you are not yet confident and practise these whenever you are asked to write something.

17 Writing to argue, persuade, advise

My learning

This section will help you to:
- concentrate on the genres of writing required in the exam
- remind you of some key features
- improve your response in the exam.

Writing to argue

Getting started

You need to know that an effective argument:
- is logical, reasonable, sensible
- is well sequenced
- has distinct stages
- may contain twists and turns
- can be balanced or one-sided, depending on the task
- needs to convince the reader.

In the exam you might be asked to argue for or against something, or you might be asked to write a balanced argument, showing both for and against.

Activity 1

Imagine you have been asked to respond to the following task:

Argue *the case for or against this proposition: 'Students should not be allowed to bring mobile phones to school'.*

1   Decide whether you are going to argue for or against and then write a list of different points you could make in the form of a list or a spidergram.
2   Number the points in your list so that they form a logical and developing argument. There will be some that link together. This will give you some links between paragraphs when you come to write your response.
3   Spend 15 minutes writing your answer.

Make sure that you begin your answer with a sentence that makes the reader want to read on to find out about the rest of your argument.

Check your answer

Make sure that you have:

- paragraphs in the best places
- links between some of the paragraphs
- correct spelling
- a range of sentence structures and some sentence forms for effect.

If not, revise your work to improve it.

Now read the following response written by a student to the same task. Then read the comments from the examiner around the response.

Clear opening, although first sentence just really repeats the task

Punctuation error

Some people say that students shouldn't be allowed to have mobile phones in school. They say that it distracts students during all their lessons, which I think is untrue because not all students do this, not many of them do. Also they say that people just steal the mobile phones but again it is untrue. There have been a few cases of it but it is starting to stop now. People also think that mobiles cost too much but there is solutions to that now because you can get phones on contracts which cost only so much a month and the phone is free!

It is ridiculous that so many people are against mobile phones when they are so useful. Nowadays 70% of teenagers own them! That's a lot of people and do you know why so many people have them? because they are useful. Mobile phones can do so many things not only can you ring people with them but they can be used as: calculators, notepads, gaming devices, alarm clocks, timers, torches, cameras, MP3 players, video players, storage devices, radios and not only can you use them for text messaging but you

Awkward phrase

Grammatical error – agreement

Energetic effective sentence

Needs capital letter

Punctuation error

Two arguments stated, though not really developed

Sentence form for effect but not made relevant to task

Rhetorical question for effect of involving the reader

Repetition of phrase reduces effectiveness

Long list effectively punctuated

Tense error

Short sentence for effect; back clearly on topic

Clear conclusion

e-mail on them now. Also say you were stuck somewhere or lost; you can ring people from anywhere you want. Also what if you were out with a friend and someone got hurt; you could easily ring for an ambulance.

The uses of mobile phones are endless so why do people not want them in schools? It is a mystery. Mobile phones should not be banned in schools at all, maybe they should put a few rules in place at most, but not ban them. They are very useful for emergencies, and there are bound to be some in a school full of teenagers. So in conclusion I don't think mobile phones should be banned in schools at all.

Not angled towards bringing phones to school; semi-colon correctly used

Needs question mark, not semi-colon

Punctuation error

The last two sentences repeat; it would have been more effective to end at 'teenagers'

What did the examiner think?

There is some good material here but:

- only some parts of the response are arguing
- not much is about bringing mobile phones into school
- the writer tends to assert rather than argue
- the list in the second paragraph is very long and not quite on topic
- the final paragraph tends to repeat what has already been said rather than take the argument a stage further.

Activity 2

Remind yourself of your answer to the same task (in response to question 3 of Activity 1). Using the sorts of points that the examiner has made above, write a list of ways you could improve your own answer.

Activities 1 and 2 were about a one-sided argument. If you were asked to write a balanced argument, showing both sides of the case, the task would be something like this:

To what extent do you agree with the proposition that students should not be allowed to bring mobile phones into school?

Activity 3

Using the new task, make a list of points you could make on the opposite side of the argument:

To what extent do you agree with the proposition that students should not be allowed to bring mobile phones into school?

Activity 4

The key to an effective answer is organisation and sequencing.

1 So, now you need to:

   - make a list of points to include for the whole of your response to the task in Activity 3

   - decide on a logical order for them

   - number your points so that the argument develops

   - jot down some discourse markers that you could use, such as 'on the other hand', 'nevertheless', 'in contrast'.

2 Now decide where you want to get to at the end of your response. Write a punchy ending that makes sure the reader stays interested right to the very end.

Writing to persuade

Getting started

You need to know that persuasive writing is characterised by:

- a range of points
- working to a clear conclusion
- some direct appeals to the reader
- some emotive language
- devices to engage the reader, such as rhetorical questions, personal anecdote
- not bullying the reader
- material closely suited to the target audience.

Read the following extracts from student responses A–D to the following task:

*Write an article for a teenage magazine in which you **persuade** the readers not to smoke.*

Then read the comments from the examiner around the first response.

Student A

I know how it feels to be gasping for a cig., but if you take your mind off it and have a distraction then it will help. Make sure you tell all your smoking friends you've stopped because I forgot when I stopped, otherwise you'll just get offered and give in if you have no will power.

Gets the reader on the writer's side – persuades

Appropriate teenage language

Positive approach helps to persuade

Personal anecdote which helps to persuade

Slightly spoiled by suggesting reader might not have any will power

Student B

Smoking leaves you really unfit and gaspin' for air, all teenagers should be able to run around and enjoy themselves at this early and prime stage of their lives, they say childhood is the most enjoyable time of life and, don't you think, smoking would ruin all that, footy in the park with the lads will never be the same again. And if that's not bad enough smoking makes you have an unpleasant smell which any amount of your favourite Calvin Klein can't shift. A smoker is easily detectable, so theres not much point trying to hide it from your parents or friends.

Student C

Some teenagers same age as me think its cool to smoke a cigarette, I don't really no why they think its cool to smoke maybe they want to fit in more, or think it's a fashinabil thing to do but to be honest I think crase has gone. Its not fashinabil to smoke these days. Thay just want attention and think the cool hard and in.

Student D

> You think it cool, you say. Or 'All my friends do it.' If your friends jump off a cliff, are you going to as well? Some teenagers smoke to ease the pressure of GCSEs and school, or some to look cool and tough in front of others. When really you're weak, your doing it to ease pressure. You should tough it out and work harder. Thinking your tough because your friends do it makes you weak. It means your giving in to peer preasure and afraid of what your social life may become.

Activity 5

1 Having read the examiner's comments on Student A, and the student responses for Students B, C and D, list:
   - the ways each uses language to persuade
   - the ways each uses sentence forms to persuade.

2 Now decide how successful the responses from Students A, B C and D are, bearing in mind the following questions.
   - How well does this response use language to persuade?
   - How well does it use sentence forms to persuade?
   - Does it concentrate on persuading (rather than informing or advising, for instance)?
   - How accurate is it in terms of spelling and punctuation?

Activity 6

1 Write two paragraphs of your own in response to this topic:
   *Write an article for a teenage magazine in which you **persuade** the readers not to smoke.*

2 Swap your completed response with a partner. Apply the following mark scheme descriptors which the examiners will be using and decide where the response has examples of the bullet points below.

Notional D	Notional C	Notional B
• conscious attempt to suit the needs of purpose and audience • begins to engage the reader's response.	• clear identification with purpose and audience • begins to sustain the reader's response.	• form, content and style are generally matched to purpose and audience.

Writing to advise

Getting started

You need to know that writing to advise is a formal kind of writing, where:

- the writer has the knowledge and the wisdom
- the reader is usually addressed directly in the second person ('you')
- the language used is usually formal
- commands are often used ('make sure you', 'take the opportunity to', 'don't', 'check')
- modals and conditionals are used ('you should', 'you ought to', 'you might like to').

Read what a student wrote in response to the following task:

*A friend of yours has been left some money. Advise him/her what to do with it. Write a letter **advising** how best to spend the money.*

Dear Mohammed,

Money comes and goes, so let's go and have some fun, eh?

But ask yourself is it the right thing to do? Why go and have some fun when we can give it to someone poor and needy? Isn't that what Islam teaches? To give money to the poor. We can have lots of fun. We don't need money. So come on, Mohammed, let's go to a mosque and give it to some people, what do you think?

Right fine you don't want to give it to a mosque. Well, let's think. You think of something. You seem to say no to everything I say.

Ohh! I have an idea. Well you know that you're a tiny bit older than me, than why don't you treat me to a football match it's something I've always wanted to see one.

No not like on the telly! Like in person, Please Mohammed, pretty, pretty please, with a cherry on top!

Just imagine you and me in some class seats shouting "REAL MADRID" for a whole 90 minutes. It would be so much fun, actually fun wouldn't be the word, because I've never been before so I actually wouldn't know. But remember this, Mohammed, if you did take me you would make a little guy over exatic, over the moon.

Ohh your mum gave it to you?

Yea so we can spend it, pretty pretty please, I'd do anything. Just think about it again, climbing all those stairs, sitting in a blue chair, with the sun looking down on us, you and me like 74,098 other people, it would make us part of one big "Real Madrid" football family, with the noise of the drums and the real football hooligans.

Then after we could go spend the rest of the money on some gear, because your dress sense is out of order! Actually we will go before the match, Mohammed, make you look nice and decent. Why knows we might or might not get some girls after the match, or even during half time. After all this it could be a memorable night, if you know what I mean. So pretty, pretty please, with another cherry on top, can we go?

Yes, wait till everyone knows about us. Yes, you and me and 74,098 others screaming our team out. Can you imagine it? That adrenalin running down from our head. I can't wait "Brother".

What did the examiner think?

This is a lively and engaging piece of writing with all kinds of positive qualities (and some errors and places where the writing could effectively be tighter). It would get a Grade C.

Activity 7

Looking again at the student's response on pages 140–1, not all of it concentrates fully on advice.

1 Jot down:
   - which parts are clearly advice
   - how language is used to advise
   - how sentence structures (and sentence forms for effect) are used.
2 Make a list of ways it could be improved.

What did the examiner think?

For a better Grade C the student's response needs to:
- concentrate more fully on advice
- cut out some of the repetition
- use a wider vocabulary
- have a bit more sense of a letter; it's a bit too much like one side of a conversation.

For a B it needs to:
- be much more focused on advice
- have a clearer structure
- use a much wider vocabulary for effect
- use more effective paragraphing
- be technically a lot more accurate.

Activity 8

Having read these comments, write on this topic for about 15 minutes with the Grade C and Grade B targets above in mind:

*A friend of yours has been left some money. Advise him/her what to do with it. Write a letter **advising** how best to spend the money.*

Bringing it all together

In the Paper 1 Section B exam, Question 6 is the last question on the paper, which you can choose to do if you like. It is a 'mixed genre' task. This means it uses two of the words in the same task. It might ask you to:

- argue and persuade
- argue and advise
- persuade and advise.

If you choose to answer Question 6:

- you don't have to write the same amount on each of the two, but make sure you have written enough on each to give the examiner plenty of material to assess your skills
- you can either do the skills separately in two sections or you can interweave them
- make sure you cover both of them adequately in the planning stage.

What have I learnt?

Check that you:

- know how to argue, persuade and advise
- can choose suitable vocabulary
- can choose suitable sentence structures and organisation
- can interest the reader by varying your vocabulary and sentence structure
- can use the mark band descriptors to make sure your work is in the higher bands.

In the future you:

- can practise these different kinds of writing
- can practise checking and improving your work for technical accuracy.

18 Writing to inform, explain, describe

My learning

This section will help you to:
- concentrate on the genres of writing required in the exam
- remind you of some key features
- improve your response in the exam.

Assessment Objectives

- Communicate clearly and imaginatively, using and adapting forms for different readers and purposes.
- Organise ideas into sentences, paragraphs and whole texts using a variety of linguistic and structural features.
- Use a range of sentence structures effectively with accurate punctuation and spelling.

Writing to inform

Getting started

You need to know that informative writing is:
- clearly organised and sequenced
- full of facts
- completely focused on the topic
- sometimes divided into sections with headings and sub-headings
- not always in continuous prose.

You might be asked to provide information on any topic and in a variety of forms. Sometimes it might be an information sheet (for parents or visitors to the area, for example). It might be in article form. It might be in the form of a report.

Activity 1

Imagine you have been asked to write an informative article on this topic:

*Many people are interested in animals. Write an **informative** article on an animal or animals of your choice.*

Before you start writing your response, the following will help you to plan it.

1   Decide whether you are going to write about one animal or more than one. If it's more than one, make sure you inform the reader about why you have chosen to tell them about more than one animal and why they should think about them together in the same article.

2   Decide who your audience will be. Many exam questions tell you what your audience is. This task doesn't, so you have to decide.

3   You know you have to inform. Decide what kind of article it is going to be. What will its audience be? What sort of newspaper or magazine do you imagine it appearing in?

4   Write a list of the different kinds of information you are going to include in the form of a list or spidergram.

5   Group your points from question 4 and decide whether you are going to have sub-headings or not. Then number them so that the reader is getting the information in a sensible order and so that you don't end up repeating yourself.

6   Now you are ready to start writing your response in full. Make sure that you begin the article with an interesting opening. You want an opening sentence that catches the readers' interest and makes them want to read on. Think of a catchy headline or leave a space to put it in later.

Spend 15 minutes writing your response.

Examiner hint

Always think before you start about:

• your purpose (here it's to inform)

• your audience (it's not stated here so you have to decide)

• your form (here it's an article, but it might be a letter or an information sheet).

Activity 2

1   Check your work to make sure you have:
   - started new paragraphs in the best places
   - correct spelling
   - a range of sentence structures and some sentence forms for effect.

   Make any necessary changes.

2   Now look at your response and a partner's to check the following.
   - Is the information well sequenced?
   - Are there links between paragraphs or sections?
   - Have you both avoided repetition?
   - Have you made sure that everything you have written is designed to inform?

Read the student response that follows, on the same topic, and look at the examiner annotations.

> I am writing to inform you about one of the
> fastest animals in the world, the cheetah. It is
> one of the most fastest and strongest animals in
> the food chain and is not eaten as prey. However
> this animal is becoming endangered of extincsion
> due to it being hunted for its skin.
>
> A cheetah is recgonised by its skin which is
> made up of very distinctive spots. It is normally
> 2 metres long and some could grow up to two
> and a half metres tall. A cheetah can move
> from standing to running extremley quickly. It
> is one of the world's most fastest accelerating
> animals. The acceleration of a cheetah is from
> 0 miles per hour to 60 miles per hour in a
> matter of seconds. This is faster than many high
> performance cars.
>
> They mainly live quite close to the equator of
> the earth as they live in very hot countries and

Annotations:
- Clear opening though not very interesting
- Grammatical error
- Spelling error
- Spelling error
- Good, varied vocabulary
- Spelling error
- Grammatical error
- Sentence variation for effect: punchy end to paragraph
- Subject needs to be stated at the beginning of new paragraph – cheetahs
- Don't need 'of the earth'

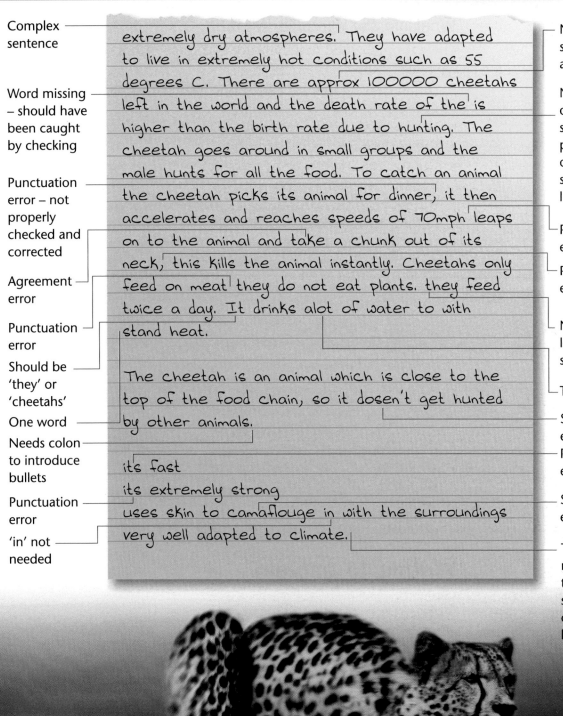

Complex sentence

extremely dry atmospheres. They have adapted to live in extremely hot conditions such as 55 degrees C. There are approx 100000 cheetahs left in the world and the death rate of the is higher than the birth rate due to hunting. The cheetah goes around in small groups and the male hunts for all the food. To catch an animal the cheetah picks its animal for dinner, it then accelerates and reaches speeds of 70mph leaps on to the animal and take a chunk out of its neck, this kills the animal instantly. Cheetahs only feed on meat they do not eat plants. they feed twice a day. It drinks alot of water to with stand heat.

The cheetah is an animal which is close to the top of the food chain, so it dosen't get hunted by other animals.

it's fast
its extremely strong
uses skin to camaflouge in with the surroundings
very well adapted to climate.

Word missing – should have been caught by checking

Punctuation error – not properly checked and corrected

Agreement error

Punctuation error

Should be 'they' or 'cheetahs'

One word

Needs colon to introduce bullets

Punctuation error

'in' not needed

Needs a full stop to show abbreviation

New aspect of topic – should be new paragraph or sentences should be linked

Punctuation error

Punctuation error

Needs capital letter to start sentence

Two words

Spelling error

Punctuation error

Spelling error

Turns into note form at the end – loses shape – no conclusion – loses structure

147

What did the examiner think?

There is much good material here and some of it is well expressed, but:

- the sentence structures could be more varied and interesting
- the opening sentence is dull
- the ending isn't very successful
- the structure could be more effective if each new aspect was in a new paragraph
- the order of the information is not always logical or helpful to the reader
- there are a lot of small errors (punctuation, capital letters, spelling, grammar).

Activity 3

Now look at your own informative article from Activities 1 and 2. Check your response using the following list and make any changes that you need to in order to improve it:

- sequencing
- paragraphs
- sentence structure
- punctuation
- spelling
- first and last sentences.

Writing to explain

Getting started

When you are writing to explain, you need to know that your response:

- is clear and logical
- gives reasons and develops them
- sees all sides of the issue
- convinces the reader of the appropriateness of the explanations.

Read what a student wrote opposite in response to the following task:

*Teenagers are often criticised in newspapers. Write a letter to the editor of a national newspaper **explaining** why this is often unfair.*

I am writing to inform you that I have a deep problem with what you put in these articles of yours, which I find very disturbing. That is about teenagers why do you criticise them? What is your problem? Yes, they do cause some problems, but at the same time there is always a reason. That could be corrupt parents, no education etc.

Do you actually think it is a teenagers who cause problems such as vandalism or problems to society. Around 40% cause this kind of problem, but there is always a reason. That could be corrupt parents, no education, etc. Those are the sort of things you should be writing about. Criticising teenagers will cause a deeper problem, will cause them to be more corrupt, they are what they are, it just cannot be helped. Teenagers through the years, have been working on charities and fund raising, they'd pretty much do anything to get what they want.

I would really want you to cut down with this nonsense, you should be writing about more serious content like what people have been going through in there everyday lives and that.

Any one would know a corrupt teenager when they see one, like we all know they would be wearing dark clothes, which could make them look scary and a part of thugs life, we would hate to be in their position, but that don't mean we can help. How about if we raise an educational fund for teenagers of a thug life, we could succeed and change their life's forever, seeing someone happy is what I've always liked. So are you with me.

Even religion can be another option - because all religions involve peace and harmony, respect as well. This is what we all want.

You will eventually be getting more letters like this, and lets hope you'd listen to what I have written to you, because this is something that should be taken care of, before further problems occur.

Thanks for listening.

Your sincerely,

A Student

What did the examiner think?

This is fairly typical of students who don't do as well as they could in the exam. This student begins to write before thinking through what they are going to say. There was no plan and therefore it just rushes from one thing to another. It gets a D.

Activity 4

Looking again at the student's response on page 149, not all of it concentrates fully on explaining why criticism of teenagers is often unfair. Jot down:

1 which parts of the student's response do explain why criticism of teenagers is often unfair

2 which parts deal with unfair criticism

3 sentences that run on from one another with commas wrongly used instead of full stops.

What did the examiner think?

For a Grade C the student response needs to:
- start with a list of points to be made that are then sequenced and linked
- focus on the unfairness of the criticism
- use a wider vocabulary
- correct the errors
- have a wider range of material.

For a Grade B it needs to:
- focus throughout on what teenagers are criticised for and why this criticism is unfair
- have a clear structure
- link points and paragraphs
- use a much wider vocabulary for effect
- use accurate and tidy sentence structures
- be a lot more technically accurate.

Activity 5

Now write on the following topic for about 15 minutes with the above Grade C and Grade B targets in mind:

*Teenagers are often criticised in newspapers. Write a letter to the editor of a national newspaper **explaining** why this is often unfair.*

Writing to describe

Getting started

You need to know that descriptive writing often makes use of:

- detail to capture what you are describing and to interest the reader
- the senses: sight, sound, smell, touch, taste
- adjectives and adverbs (though not overused)
- the desire to let the reader know exactly what something was like.

Read extracts A–D from some student responses to the following task:

Describe *your home.*

Then read the comments from the examiner around the first response.

Student A

Detail and adjective; use of smell

Unusual word for interest

Three simple adjectives

Two adjectives – sight

Two adjectives – smell

> As I enter the kitchen for breakfast, I smell the burnt toast left over from brother Bill. I hear the penetration 'Wack!' 'Wack' from next doors builders, building one of those nice new modern glass extensions like the ones you see on holiday in Spain.
>
> Greeted by my big fluffy dog with his warm musky breath heaving on the back of my leg, I give him a stroke, he thinks it's a joke.

Detail of another aspect of home introduced

Sound; onomatopoeia

Does more than list contents – makes reader imagine

Rhyme to entertain the reader

Student B

When you go up the stairs, there is the best room in front of you – my room. In my small bedroom, there is a comfortable double-bed in front of you, a television and playstation 2 in the far corner and two wardrobes by the doorway. If you go into the room next door there is my mum's bedroom, which just has a bed, lots of wardrobes and a treadmill, which she never uses. If you carry on walking through the L-shaped landing, there is my little sisters bedroom. Next to that, is the small bathroom which has just enough space for a bathtub, toilet and sink.

Student C

It does not matter how much big or small your home is, as long as you have got one and you live in it. I like my home because it is big and there is enough space for everyone. I lived in a 2 bedroom house 1 year before I moved to my new house. I have fashionable and designable curtains in every room especially made from Pakistan. I have got big vases with colourful artificial flowers in them. This is my home!!!

Student D

My bedroom, the place where the real magic happens. The situation of my room is underneath the highest slate on my roof, the loft. In my head it's my Penthouse. The staircase that winds up to it, from the first floor remind me of myself, fun, confusing and wild. They ruin the conventions of any other bring, normal staircase. They wind. Like me. The colour of my room represents the most important time of anyone's life …. Their childhood. Those were the days, when soil looked good enough to eat and there was no harm in having your mummy or your teddy as your best friend. Long live pink.

Activity 6

1 Having read the student responses on pages 151 and 152, and the examiner's comments on Student A, for Students B, C and D, list:
   - the ways each uses language to describe
   - the ways each uses sentence forms to describe
   - the ways they do more than just make a list of contents, but show what things are like.

2 Now decide how successful the responses from Students A, B, C and D are, bearing in mind the following questions.
   - How well do they use language to describe?
   - How well do they use sentence forms to describe?
   - How well do they concentrate on describing (rather than informing, for instance)?

Activity 7

1 Write two paragraphs of your own in response to this topic:
   Describe *your home.*

2 Swap your completed response with a partner and apply the following mark scheme descriptors which the examiners will be using. Highlight places where you could make improvements and decide where the response has examples of the bullet points below.

Notional D	Notional C	Notional B
• conscious attempt to suit the needs of purpose and audience • begins to engage the reader's response.	• clear identification with purpose and audience • begins to sustain the reader's response.	• form, content and style are generally matched to purpose and audience.

Bringing it all together

In the Paper 2 Section B exam, Question 6 is the last question on the paper, which you can choose to do if you like. It is a 'mixed genre' task. This means it uses two of the words in the same task. It might ask you to:

- inform and describe
- inform and explain
- describe and explain.

If you choose to answer Question 6:

- you don't have to write the same amount on each of the two, but make sure you have written enough on each to give the examiner plenty of material to assess your skills
- you can either do the skills separately in two sections or you can interweave them
- make sure you cover both of them adequately in the planning stage.

What have I learnt?

Check that you:

- know how to write for these different key words
- can choose suitable vocabulary
- can choose suitable sentence structures and organisation
- can interest the reader by varying your vocabulary and sentence structure
- can use the mark band descriptors to make sure your work is in the higher bands.

In the future you:

- can practise these different kinds of writing
- can practise checking your work for key features
- can practise checking and improving your work for technical accuracy.

Exam practice

Paper 1: Foundation

PAPER 1: FOUNDATION

SECTION A: READING

Answer **all** questions in this section.

You are advised to spend about one hour on this section.

---

1   Read Item 1, the news report called 'India Official Dies After Monkey Attack'.

   (a) Select and write down **two** facts and **two** opinions from Item 1, 'India
        Official Dies After Monkey Attack'.   (*4 marks*)

   (b) According to this Item, what are the problems with monkeys and the
        problems in controlling the monkeys?   (*5 marks*)

Now look at both Item 1, 'India Official Dies After Monkey Attack', and Item 2
'Drunken Monkey Killed my Wife!' together.

   (c) Compare the ways the two Items present someone's death after an attack
        by monkeys.   (*6 marks*)

2   Now return to Item 2, 'Drunken Monkey Killed my Wife!'

   (a) How does the writer use language to make the article dramatic? (*6 marks*)

   (b) How are presentational devices used in this Item to make the reader
        interested?   (*6 marks*)

Item 1

Associated Press

Related News

New Delhi's deputy mayor killed
News Today – 2 hours ago

Monkey kills deputy mayor
India on-line – 6 hours ago

Deputy mayor killed by monkey
Asia.com – 8 hours ago

Full coverage »

India Official Dies After Monkey Attack

1 day ago

New Delhi (AP) – Wild monkeys attacked a senior government official who then fell from a balcony at his home and died Sunday, media reported.

New Delhi Deputy Mayor S.S. Bajwa was rushed to hospital after the attack by a gang of Rhesus macaques, but succumbed to head injuries sustained in his fall, the Press Trust of India news agency and The Times of India reported.

Many government buildings, temples and residential neighbourhoods in New Delhi are overrun by Rhesus macaques, which scare passers-by and occasionally bite or snatch food from unsuspecting visitors.

Last year, the Delhi High Court reprimanded authorities for failing to stop the animals from terrifying residents and asked them to find a permanent solution to the monkey menace.

Part of the problem is that devout Hindus believe monkeys are manifestations of the monkey god Hanuman and feed them bananas and peanuts – encouraging them to frequent public places.

Over the years, city authorities have employed monkey catchers who use langurs – a larger and fiercer kind of monkey – to scare or catch the macaques, but the problem persists.

Item 2

Daily Sport   Monday, October 30, 2006   **11**

DRUNKEN MONKEY KILLED MY WIFE!

■ by NEIL GOODWIN

A WOMAN has died after a drunken monkey lobbed a brick at her head from the top of a building site.

Mala Manhas, 30, was on her way to visit a sick nephew in hospital as she walked past the construction site in New Delhi.

Sitting on scaffolding on the eighth floor was a rhesus macaque monkey which was blind-drunk after scoffing fermented apples in a nearby orchard.

Inquiry

And Mala suffered horrific head injuries as the pissed-up primate aimed a concrete missile at her skull.

She was rushed to the nearby hospital's emergency ward, but died from her injuries.

Husband Ranjit, from nearby Meethapur, has called for an inquiry.

The 32-year-old widower said: 'I am devastated at what has happened to poor Mala, and I want that monkey found and shot.

'We were about to visit our nephew Rahul, who has dengue fever, and it was already a very sad day for us.

'Now I am without a wife, all because a monkey was so drunk he threw rocks and bricks at people.

'I urge the hospital authorities to take urgent action.

He added: 'If needs be, the monkeys should all be poisoned and killed.'

157

SECTION B: WRITING TO ARGUE, PERSUADE OR ADVISE

Answer **one** question from this section.

You are advised to spend about 45 minutes on this section.

You may use some of the information from Section A if you want to, but you do not have to do so.
If you use any of the information, do **not** simply copy it.

Remember:
- spend 5 minutes planning and sequencing your material
- try to write at least one side in your answer book
- spend 5 minutes checking:
  - your paragraphing
  - your punctuation
  - your spelling.

EITHER

3   Write a letter to a newspaper editor, for publication in the paper, **arguing** for *or* against the idea that people and animals should be kept well away from each other.

You might write about:
- how well humans get on with animals
- the dangers or attractions of being with animals
- what you think about relationships between people and animals.

Remember to:
- argue for or against
- use the right language for a newspaper.   (*27 marks*)

OR

4   Write an article for your local newspaper **explaining** how and why your neighbourhood can be made a pleasanter place to live in.

You might write about:
- how your neighbourhood could be improved
- reasons for improving your neighbourhood.

Remember to:
- write to explain
- write for your local newspaper.   (*27 marks*)

OR

5   Write an advice sheet for people your own age, **advising** them how to make the most of the year in which they sit their GCSE exams.

You might write about:
- how to organise their work
- how to organise their leisure time
- how to use resources available to them.

Remember to:
- write an advice sheet
- write for people your own age
- use the right language for advising.   (*27 marks*)

OR

6   Write an article for your school or college magazine **informing** readers about the dangers of being overweight and **advising** them how they can avoid this.

You might write about:
- the dangers of being overweight
- the disadvantages of being overweight
- what they could do about it
- why they should do something about it.

Remember to:
- write an article
- write for your school or college magazine
- write to inform and advise.   (*27 marks*)

Exam practice

Paper 1: Higher

PAPER 1: HIGHER

SECTION A: READING

Answer **all** questions in this section.

You are advised to spend about one hour on this section.

---

1   Read Item 1, a newspaper report from *The Daily Sport* called 'Drunken Monkey Killed my Wife!'

(a) How are facts and opinions used in Item 1?   (*5 marks*)

Now read Item 2, the web page entitled 'Delhi battles with monkey menace'.

(b) What differing attitudes towards monkeys are shown in these two Items?

(*8 marks*)

2   Now return to Item 1, 'Drunken Monkey Killed my Wife!'

(a) How does the writer use language to make the story sensational and dramatic?

(*6 marks*)

Now look at both Items together.

(b) How are presentational devices used to make these two Items attractive and
     interesting to the reader?   (*8 marks*)

Item 1

Daily Sport Monday, October 30, 2006 **11**

DRUNKEN MONKEY KILLED MY WIFE!

■ **by NEIL GOODWIN**

A WOMAN has died after a drunken monkey lobbed a brick at her head from the top of a building site.

Mala Manhas, 30, was on her way to visit a sick nephew in hospital as she walked past the construction site in New Delhi.

Sitting on scaffolding on the eighth floor was a rhesus macaque monkey which was blind-drunk after scoffing fermented apples in a nearby orchard.

Inquiry

And Mala suffered horrific head injuries as the pissed-up primate aimed a concrete missile at her skull.

She was rushed to the nearby hospital's emergency ward, but died from her injuries.

Husband Ranjit, from nearby Meethapur, has called for an inquiry.

The 32-year-old widower said: 'I am devastated at what has happened to poor Mala, and I want that monkey found and shot.

'We were about to visit our nephew Rahul, who has dengue fever, and it was already a very sad day for us.

'Now I am without a wife, all because a monkey was so drunk he threw rocks and bricks at people.

'I urge the hospital authorities to take urgent action.

He added: 'If needs be, the monkeys should all be poisoned and killed.'

Item 2

Make Homepage | Site Map | Desktop Ticker | RSS | Newsletter

.:: PLAYING NOW

Home | Nation | World | Sports | Business | Recipes | Lifestyle | Movies | Music | Books | Flashback | Columns | My News | Rover | V

NDTV : Q2 FY08 Results   Last updat

.:: Top Stories   Colombo: 29 killed as LTTE attacks air force base from land and air in northern Sri Lanka   Search:

NATION

✉ E-mail   🖨 Print   📹 Video   🖼 Pics   💬 Comments   📰 Forums

Most Read Stories

- Jawan arrested for killing teacher
- Blasts case: Dutt gets breather
- Left asks govt to declare N-deal is off
- Child left to rot in chains in Kerala

Poll Centre

Q. Does the success of Indian Diaspora affect the nation?

- Yes
- No
- Can't say

[VOTE]

Most Watched Videos

Delhi battles monkey menace

Stage set for crucial UPA-Left meet

Displaced tribals rue govt projects

Interactive

- **Forums**
- **Hot Debates**
- **Movie Reviews**
- **Poetry Corner**
- **SMS NDTV**

NDTV Verticals

- **Profit**
- **Travel**
- **Recipes**
- **Gadgets**
- **Movies**
- **Music**
- **Books**
- **Health**
- **Shopping**

Delhi battles monkey menace

Rate the Story

★ ★ ★ ★ ★

SMS NDTV

For latest headlines SMS **NEWS** to **56388** (in India) **6388** (in UAE), to **63880** (in UK)

Also Read

- Pranab to attend summit in China
- Lethal similarity between terror strikes
- Sanjay Dutt trudges back to prison
- N-deal to bring country to mainstream: Sharma

Alok Pandey

Monday, October 22, 2007 (New Delhi)

People living in Delhi have grappled with the monkey menace for many years now and over the past decade things have gone from bad to worse.

Delhi's Deputy Mayor S S Bajwa had to pay with his life for the capital's dreaded monkey menace.

Over the last decade or so shrinking natural habitat has saddled Delhi with an estimated 10,000 monkeys. So far, relocating them outside the city has been a colossal failure.

The monkey menace is at its worst in the areas of Lutyens Delhi, Patparganj, Anand Vihar, Mehrauli, Kamla Nagar, and also Noida and Gurgaon in the National Capital region.

Both the Municipal Corporation of Delhi and the Delhi government are responsible for keeping the simian population in check. But neither repeated reminders from the high court or the Supreme Court have made them come up with a solution to the problem.

In 2002, the Delhi High Court first took note of the monkey problem. The MCD spent Rs 14 lakh on shelters in Rajokri and Bakhtawarpur on the outskirts of Delhi and 400 odd monkeys were caught but all of them escaped from the shelters.

In 2004, the High Court ordered monkeys be relocated to Madhya Pradesh. The central government even released Rs 25 lakh to Madhya Pradesh but after receiving the first batch of 250 monkeys, the MP government demanded more money.

The case is now in Supreme Court.

This year in February, the Delhi High court directed the monkeys be sent to the Asola Bhati sanctuary on the City's outskirts. The MCD says it is finding it difficult to find catchers .

The MCD also hired langurs to scare away the monkeys. The plan failed as the scared monkeys only relocated to other areas of the city.

Now that the menace has claimed a high profile life, authorities say it is high time there is some action.

In the latest effort, a team of monkey catchers from Tamil Nadu have been offered Rs 450 for each monkey caught. And till the team reports some success, People in Delhi will have to grapple with a pest who has been growing bolder by the years.

Story Finder [   ]   2007 ▮   Go

➕ My Yahoo   Digg it   ⌂ reditt   ■ Del.icio.us   📄 Newsvine

User Comments [+Comment on the story]

Latest Comments

- The monkeys should be exported not to MP or Uttarakhand, as that will be unfairly passing on the problem to others who do not have a solution. But these can be sent to Nagaland (or the Far East) where the local people have no problem dealing with monkeys: they will eat them.
  Posted by sonja de at 11:56 on Oct 22, 2007

About Us | Feedback | Disclaimer | Investor | Careers | Transmission

SECTION B: WRITING TO ARGUE, PERSUADE OR ADVISE

Answer **one** question from this section.

You are advised to spend about 45 minutes on this section.

You may use some of the information from Section A if you want to, but you do not have to do so.
If you use any of the information, do **not** simply copy it.

Remember:
- spend 5 minutes planning and sequencing your material
- try to write at least one side in your answer book
- spend 5 minutes checking:
  - your paragraphing
  - your punctuation
  - your spelling.

EITHER

3   Write a letter to a newspaper editor, for publication in the paper, **arguing** that people and animals should be kept well away from each other.   (*27 marks*)

OR

4   Write an article for your local newspaper **explaining** how and why your neighbourhood can be made a pleasanter place to live in.   (*27 marks*)

OR

5   Write an advice sheet for people your own age, **advising** them how to make the most of the year in which they sit their GCSE exams.   (*27 marks*)

OR

6   Write an article for your school or college magazine **informing** readers about the dangers of being overweight and **advising** them how they can avoid this.

          (*27 marks*)

Exam practice

Paper 2: Foundation

PAPER 2: FOUNDATION

SECTION A: READING
POETRY FROM DIFFERENT CULTURES

This section relates to Section 1 of the *AQA Anthology* labelled *2005 onwards* that you have been using during the course.

Answer one question from this section on the poems you have studied in Section 1 of the *Anthology*: Poems from Different Cultures (pages 5–18).

You are advised to spend about 45 minutes on this section.

EITHER

1 Compare the methods used by the poets to reveal what they have to say about people and society in 'Nothing's Changed' and **one** other poem of your choice.

Write about:
- ideas about people in the two poems
- ideas about society in the two poems
- similarities in the methods the poets use
- differences in the methods the poets use. (*27 marks*)

OR

2 Compare the ways the poets use language to present their ideas in '*from* Unrelated Incidents' and **one** other poem of your choice.

- the different kinds of language in the two poems
- the ideas in the two poems
- similarities in the ways the poets use language to present their ideas
- differences in the ways the poets use language to present their ideas. (*27 marks*)

SECTION B: WRITING TO INFORM, EXPLAIN OR DESCRIBE

Answer **one** question in this section.

You are advised to spend about 45 minutes on this section.

Remember:
- spend 5 minutes planning and sequencing your material
- try to write at least one side in your answer book
- spend 5 minutes checking:
  - your paragaphing
  - your punctuation
  - your spelling.

EITHER

3   Write an article for a newspaper to **inform** adult readers about healthy living.
Remember to:
- write an article
- write for adult readers
- write about healthy living.   (*27 marks*)

OR

4   **Explain** how to get on well with the people you live with.
Remember to:
- write to explain
- write about getting on with the people you live with.   (*27 marks*)

OR

5   **Describe** a shopping centre during the daytime and at night.
Remember to:
- write to describe
- describe a shopping centre
- describe it during the daytime
- describe it at night.   (*27 marks*)

OR

6   **Describe** somewhere you dislike and **explain** why you dislike it.
Remember to:
- write to describe
- describe somewhere you dislike
- write to explain
- explain why you dislike the place.   (*27 marks*)

Exam practice

Paper 2: Higher

PAPER 2: HIGHER

SECTION A: READING
POETRY FROM DIFFERENT CULTURES

This section relates to Section 1 of the *AQA Anthology* labelled *2005 onwards* that you have been using during the course.

Answer one question from this section on the poems you have studied in Section 1 of the *Anthology*: Poems from Different Cultures (pages 5–18).

You are advised to spend about 45 minutes on this section.

EITHER

1   Compare the methods used by the poets to reveal what they have to say about people and society in 'Nothing's Changed' and **one** other poem of your choice.

(27 marks)

OR

2   Compare the ways the poets use non-standard English to present their ideas in '*from* Unrelated Incidents' and **one** other poem of your choice.   *(27 marks)*

SECTION B: WRITING TO INFORM, EXPLAIN OR DESCRIBE

Answer **one** question in this section.

You are advised to spend about 45 minutes on this section.

Remember:
- spend 5 minutes planning and sequencing your material
- try to write about two sides in your answer book
- spend 5 minutes checking:
  - your paragraphing
  - your punctuation
  - your spelling.

EITHER

3 Write an article for a newspaper to **inform** adult readers about healthy living.

(*27 marks*)

OR

4 **Explain** how to get on well with the people you live with.   (*27 marks*)

OR

5 **Describe** a shopping centre during the daytime and at night.   (*27 marks*)

OR

6 **Describe** somewhere you dislike and **explain** why you dislike it.   (*27 marks*)